OOP DEMYSTIFIED

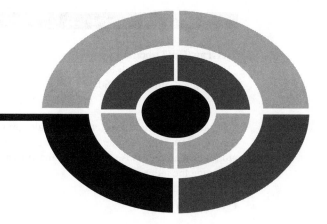

OOP DEMYSTIFIED

JAMES KEOGH
& MARIO GIANNINI

McGraw-Hill/Osborne

New York   Chicago   San Francisco   Lisbon   London
Madrid   Mexico City   Milan   New Delhi   San Juan
Seoul   Singapore   Sydney   Toronto

The McGraw·Hill Companies

McGraw-Hill/Osborne
2100 Powell Street, 10th Floor
Emeryville, California 94608
U.S.A.

To arrange bulk purchase discounts for sales promotions, premiums, or fund-raisers, please contact **McGraw-Hill**/Osborne at the above address. For information on translations or book distributors outside the U.S.A., please see the International Contact Information page immediately following the index of this book.

OOP Demystified

34567890 FGR FGR 0198765

ISBN 0-07-225363-0

Publisher Brandon A. Nordin	**Proofreader** Marian Selig
Vice President & Associate Publisher Scott Rogers	**Indexer** Claire Splan
Editorial Director Wendy Rinaldi	**Composition** Tara A. Davis, Lucie Ericksen
Project Editor Jennifer Malnick	**Illustrators** Kathleen Edwards, Melinda Lytle
Acquisitions Coordinator Athena Honore	**Cover Series Design** Margaret Webster-Shapiro
Technical Editor Jeff Kent	**Cover Illustration** Lance Lekander
Copy Editor Bart Reed	

This book was composed with Corel VENTURA™ Publisher.

*This book is dedicated to Anne, Sandy, Joanne,
Amber-Leigh Christine, and Graaf, without whose
help and support this book couldn't be written.
—Jim*

*For my son, Nicholas, whose inquisitive mind
and endless smile reminds me what it's all about.
—Mario*

ABOUT THE AUTHORS

Jim Keogh is a member of the faculty of Columbia University, where he teaches courses on Java Application Development, and is a member of the Java Community Process Program. He developed the first e-commerce track at Columbia and became its first chairperson. Jim spent more than a decade developing advanced systems for major Wall Street firms and is also the author of several best-selling computer books.

Mario Giannini is the President of Code Fighter, Inc., co-author of *Windows Programming Programmers Notebook*, and Chair of the Software Development Program at Columbia University's Information Technology Programs. With over 20 years of software development experience on CP/M, Unix, and Windows, he feels lucky to be fascinated with the ever-changing field of software development after all these years.

CONTENTS AT A GLANCE

CONTENTS

CONTENTS

INTRODUCTION

This book is for everyone who wants to learn object-oriented programming without taking a formal course. It is also designed as a supplemental classroom text. Start at the beginning of this book and then go straight through to the end for best results.

If you are confident about the topics covered in these chapters, then take the quiz at the end of each one to see if you actually know the material before skipping any chapter.

If you get 90 percent of the answers correct, skip the chapter. If you get 75 to 89 percent correct, skim through the text of chapter. If you get less than 75 percent of the answers correct, find a quiet place and begin reading. Doing so will get you in shape to tackle the rest of the chapters on object-oriented programming.

In order to learn object-oriented programming, you must have some computer skills, but don't be intimidated. None of the knowledge you need goes beyond basic computer know-how.

This book contains a lot of practice quizzes and exam questions, which are similar to the kinds of questions used in an object-oriented programming course. You may and should refer to the chapter texts when taking them. When you think you're ready, take the quiz, write down your answers, and then give your list of answers to a friend. Have your friend tell you your score, but not which questions were wrong. Stay with one chapter until you pass the quiz. You'll find the answers in Appendix B.

There is a final exam at the end of this book, in Appendix A, which contains practical questions drawn from all chapters of this book. Take the exam when you have finished the book and have completed all the quizzes. A satisfactory score is at least 75 percent. Have a friend tell you your score without letting you know which questions you missed.

We recommend that you spend an hour or two each day and expect to complete one chapter each week. Take it at a steady pace; take time to absorb the material. Don't rush. You'll complete the course in a few months; then you can use this book as a comprehensive permanent reference.

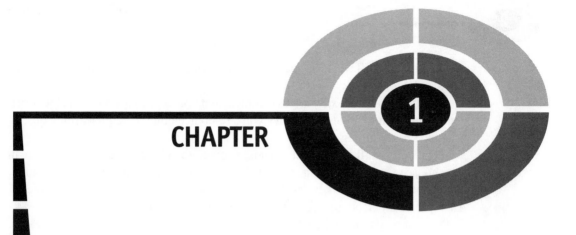

CHAPTER 1

A Look at How We See the World

How do you see the world? The answer depends on your background. A scientist might see the world as molecular structures. An artist sees the world as shapes and colors. And some of us might say the world is a collection of stuff. Probably the first thing that came to mind when you read this question was, What does it matter how anyone sees the world? It matters a lot to a programmer who has to write a computer program that emulates the real world.

The Stuff That Stuff Is Made Of

Comedian George Carlin sums up how most of us see the world in his famous comedy routine. Carlin says we see the world as stuff, and he is probably right. Stuff is anything you have and anything you want. A house is stuff. Things you have in your house are stuff. Things you throw away are stuff, and so are the things you want

to buy. And the stuff we have, such as a house, is made up of other stuff, such as windows and doors.

Admittedly the term *stuff* is less technical that you expect in a book on object-oriented programming, but it does give you a reference point to begin learning object-oriented programming.

Technically, stuff is an object. That is, a house is an object. The things you have in your house are objects. Things your throw away are objects, and things you want to buy are objects. All of us, regardless of our background, view the world as objects. An *object* is a person, place, thing, concept, or possibly event.

The best way to learn about objects is to examine the most important object, us. Each of us is considered an object in the world of object-oriented programming. We call this object a *person*.

A person as well as a house, car, and any other real-world objects are described by using two groups of features: attributes and behaviors. An *attribute* is a characteristic of an object. For example, a person has a first name, last name, height, and weight. First name, last name, height, and weight are attributes of all persons. As you can imagine, hundreds of other attributes characterize a person, but we'll stop at four. A *behavior* is an action that an object is capable of performing. A person sits, stands, walks, and runs, among thousands of other behaviors a person performs.

You can probably imagine how an automobile, airplane, and even a sales order form are objects, each having attributes and behavior. Attributes and behaviors of an automobile and airplane are fairly obvious. Both have width, height, weight, wheels, an engine, and many other attributes. An automobile and airplane move in a direction, stop, are steered to a different direction, and can perform hundreds of other actions (behaviors).

However, you might be scratching your head trying to determine the attributes and behaviors of a sales order form (see Figure 1-1). Its attributes are customer name, customer address, item ordered, amount due, and other pieces of information found on a sales order form. Its behaviors include collecting information, modifying information, and processing the sales order.

Abstract Objects and Instances

Throughout this book, you'll see how programmers view an object in two ways—as an abstract object and as a real object. The term *abstract object* can seem a bit, let's say, abstract to understand. Think of an abstract object as a description of a real object minus details. For example, an abstract person is a description of a person that contains attributes and behaviors. Here are four attributes that might be found in an

TO: Bob Jones
555 Fifth Street
Fifth Floor
New York, New York 10022

ORDER

Customer Number: 1234567

P.O. Number	Date Shipped	Shipped Via	Required Date	Terms
AC34	9/15/99	UPS	10/5/99	30 days

Quantity	Item ID	Item Name	Unit Price	Amount
4	31	Towels	$10.00	$ 40.00
3	27	Shirts	$25.00	$ 75.00

Subtotal	$115.00
Sales Tax	$ 0.00
Shipping & Handling	$ 4.50
Total Due	$119.50

Figure 1-1   An order form is an object that contains attributes and behaviors.

abstract person (notice that these attributes simply identify a kind of characteristic, such as first name or weight, but don't specify a name or measurement):

- First Name
- Last Name
- Height
- Weight

The abstract object is used as the model for a real object. A real person has all the attributes and behaviors defined in the abstract object and contains details missing from the abstract object.

For example, the abstract person is a model for a real person. The abstract person states that a real person must have a first name, last name, height, and weight. A real person specifies values associated with these attributes, such as:

- Bob
- Smith
- 6 feet tall
- 160 pounds

As you'll see in later chapters, programmers create an abstract object and then use the abstract object to create a real object. A real object is called an *instance* of the abstract object. You can say that a real person is an instance of the abstract person.

Some programmers like to think of an abstract object as a cookie cutter. A cookie cutter shaped as a cookie, but isn't a cookie. You might say that a cookie cutter is an abstract cookie used to define what a real cookie looks like. A cookie cutter is used to cut out real cookies from a sheet of dough. That is, a cookie cutter is used to create instances of a cookie.

Why an Object?

By now you're wondering what is so revolutionary about looking at the world as objects. The short answer is that focusing on objects makes it easy for us to understand complex things. Objects enable us to look at details that are of interest to us and ignore other details that we are not interested in.

This is evident when you meet your teacher. A teacher is a person and has many of the attributes and behaviors that you posses. Yet, you probably ignore many of the teacher's attributes and behaviors and focus on only those that pertain to your education.

Likewise, the teacher focuses on your attributes and behaviors that indicate how well you are learning material in class. Other attributes, such as your performance in an unrelated class or your height and weight, are ignored by the teacher. Similarly, a teacher may not care if you drive a car or walk to campus.

Both you and your teacher simplify your relationship by deciding attributes and behaviors that are important to each of your objectives and then use only those attributes and behaviors in your relationship.

Inheritance

Inheritance is an important feature of object-oriented programming because it is a way for one object to receive attributes and behaviors of another object in what programmers call an "is a" relationship. As an example, let's use the Person and Student objects to discuss how inheritance works.

Previously in this chapter, you learned that Person has many attributes and behaviors. In this example, we'll limit Person's attributes and behaviors to those shown in Table 1-1.

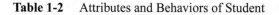

Attributes	Behaviors
First Name	Sitting
Last Name	Standing
Address	Walking
Telephone Number	Running

Table 1-1   Attributes and Behaviors of Person

Student has the same attributes and behaviors as Person because Student is a person. In addition, Student has attributes and behaviors that are unique to a student. Some of these are shown in Table 1-2.

Attributes	Behaviors
Student Number	Taking a test
Major	Attending class
Grade Point Average	Doing homework

Table 1-2   Attributes and Behaviors of Student

It makes sense that Student inherits attributes and behaviors of Person because Student has an "is a" relationship with Person. That is, a student is a person. You'll learn how to define objects in Chapter 2 and how objects are inherited in Chapter 5. For now, let's consider Table 1-1 as the definition of Person and Table 1-2 as the definition of Student.

Table 1-1 and Table 1-2 simply define Person and Student, but they don't create a real person or real student. For that, you need to create an instance of Person or Student. An instance is a real object. Therefore, an instance of Person is a real person, and an instance of Student is a real student.

Once Student inherits from Person, an instance of Student has the attributes and behaviors of Person and Student, just as if all attributes and behaviors were defined in Student. Table 1-3 shows the attributes and behaviors of an instance of Student after Student inherits from Person.

This means that a programmer who creates only an instance of Student can access attributes and behaviors of Person without creating an instance of Person. The programmer accesses attributes and behaviors of Person by using the instance of Student.

Attributes	Behaviors
First Name	Sitting
Last Name	Standing
Address	Walking
Telephone Number	Running
Student Number	Taking a test
Major	Attending class
Grade Point Average	Doing homework

Table 1-3   Attributes and Behaviors Available to an Instance of Student

Why Use Inheritance?

Maintaining objects can become a nightmare for programmers, as you'll quickly discover once you start creating your own object-oriented programs. Real-world programs require many objects, each having many attributes and behaviors. It becomes your responsibility to organize these objects so you can easily change them as requirements for your program change.

Here's the dilemma: Let's say you don't define a Person object. Instead, attributes and behaviors that would normally be defined in a Person object (refer to Table 1-1) are placed in objects that are persons. These objects are Student, Teacher, Department Chair, Dean, Secretary, and Bursar. In other words, attributes and behaviors listed in Table 1-1 are repeated six times, once for each of the six objects.

Now for the problem: You need to insert a Cell Phone attribute. It makes sense to insert the Cell Phone attribute in the Person object because many people have cell phones, but the Person object isn't defined. The only solution is to insert the Cell Phone attribute into all six objects.

Real-world programmers don't do this because they know to group together into one object those attributes and behaviors that are common to multiple objects. In this example, common attributes and behaviors of a person are defined in the Person object. The other five objects inherit the Person object and its attributes and behaviors.

Inserting the Cell Phone attribute becomes an easy task because the change is made to one object—the Person object. The other objects automatically receive the Cell Phone attribute when they inherit the Person object.

Objects in the Business World

You will find yourself using objects that are common in business to build an object-oriented business system. Let's take a look at a supermarket to get a better understanding of a business system and the objects used in business (see Figure 1-2). You've visited plenty of supermarkets, so you probably have a general idea of how a supermarket receives merchandise from a warehouse.

Each week supermarket employees survey the shelves and the storeroom to determine what products to order from the supermarket's central warehouse. They place information about each product and the quantity to order on an order form, which then is sent to the warehouse for fulfillment.

At the warehouse, information on the order form is transferred to a pick list used by warehouse employees while going through the warehouse "picking" products to fill the order. Products are listed on a packing slip and then placed in cartons. A packing slip lists all the products contained in the carton and their quantities. A shipping label is placed on a carton, and a shipping order is written. The shipping order has instructions on where the cartons are to be delivered. A trucker then uses the shipping order to deliver the carton to the supermarket.

Employees in the supermarket read the label on each carton to be sure that the carton is addressed to them. They open the carton and read the packing slip. Items on the packing slip are compared to items in the carton. Any discrepancies are noted and reported to the warehouse in a memo. Items are then removed from the carton and placed on supermarket shelves.

There are many objects in the system a supermarket uses to order merchandise to restock shelves. These include an employee, a building, cartons, and a truck. However, we are interested in objects of the system, such as the form used to order merchandise.

What business objects do you see in the supermarket ordering system? Time's up! Compare your list of objects to this list:

- Order form
- Pick list
- Packing slip
- Shipping order
- Shipping label

Each object has attributes and behaviors. Attributes include the product number, product name, and quantity, which are found in each of these objects, except for the shipping label. Attributes of the shipping label object include the name and address of the supermarket and the name and address of the shipper.

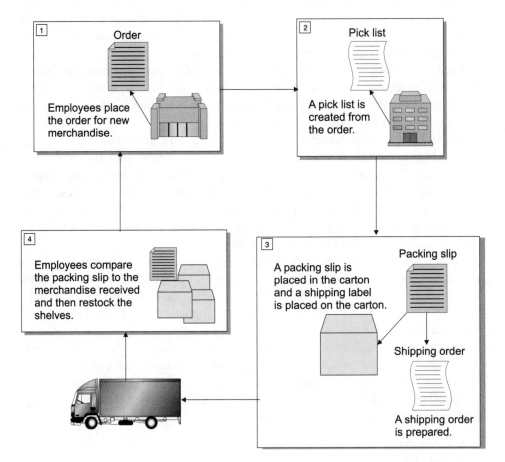

Figure 1-2 A supermarket uses a business system and business objects to restock shelves with merchandise.

Many objects used in business are forms that someone fills out, such as an order form. It is hard to imagine an object having a behavior because it doesn't do anything. It is not like a window that opens and closes.

However, an object *does* have behaviors. Here are a few behaviors of an order form object:

- Enter information
- Modify information
- Delete modified information
- Display the form
- Process the order
- Modify the order
- Cancel the order

Real-Life Objects and Object-Oriented Programming

For decades, programmers have undertaken the enormous job of writing computer programs that automate the way business is conducted. In the "olden days," as some programmers might say, a program consisted of one long series of step-by-step instructions that directed the computer to do something. Typically programs were used to automate a business process such as processing an order, which is the same thing that programs do today.

Once the automation fever caught on, businesses demanded that programs take over many business operations. Programs grew in size and complexity and soon became unmanageable, expensive, and time consuming to maintain.

Procedural programming came to rescue programmers. Procedural programming organizes instructions into groups that perform one task, called a *procedure*. Procedures are referred to as *functions* or *methods* in some programming languages. Think of a procedure as instructions used to enter a new order, display an existing order, or perform any task.

Procedural programming simplified programming by making it easy for a programmer to quickly sift through hundreds of lines of instructions to locate a procedure that needed to be upgraded.

In addition, procedural programming provided another benefit that made a programmer's life more bearable. Procedures, written in a programming language such as C, can be reused in other programs that require the same procedures. Programmers refer to this as *reusable code*.

Here's how reusable code works: Let's say that a programmer writes a procedure in an order-processing program that matches a ZIP code with a city and state. This enables a sales representative to enter a customer's ZIP code and then let the computer look up the city and state associated with the ZIP code.

You can imagine that many programs within a company have the same need. Rather than rewrite the ZIP code procedure for each of those programs, a programmer can use the same ZIP code procedure in those programs. This saves time and money, and it produces reliable programs because the ZIP code procedure is already thoroughly tested.

Procedural programming revolutionized how programs were written, but there was another problem that still needed to be addressed. The real world, which a program mimics, is organized into objects, and not procedures. An object consists of attributes and behaviors, as you know.

Each time a new program was written, the programmer had the challenge of re-creating an object-oriented world using a procedural programming language. It was like trying to slip an octagonal peg into a round hole. The peg fits with a little coaxing, but it's never a perfect fit.

The problem was solved with the introduction of object-oriented programming in the 1980s. Object-oriented programming uses an object-oriented programming language such as C++ or Java to mimic real-world objects in a program by defining a class. A *class* is composed of data members and member methods. *Data members* are sometimes referred to as *fields* and are used to store attributes of an object. *Member methods* are sometimes referred to as *member functions* and define an object's behavior. You'll learn much more about classes throughout chapters of this book.

Quiz

1. What is an object?

2. What is an attribute of an object?

3. What is a behavior of an object?

4. Why it is important for programmers to use object-oriented programming to develop computer systems?

5. Explain the role of inheritance in object-oriented programming.

6. How can object-oriented programming help maintain complex computer systems?

7. Identify the attributes of the order form in Figure 1-1.

8. Identify the behaviors of the order form in Figure 1-1.

9. Describe objects in a college that might inherit a Person object.

10. Draw a diagram that shows the relationships of objects that you listed in your answer to Question 9.

What Is a Class?

How can you squeeze four students inside a computer? The answer is, by using a series of zeros and ones. That wasn't the punch line you expected to hear, but it is true. Computers view students—and the world—as a bunch of zeros and ones, collectively called *data*. And clever programmers manipulate data to represent real-world objects by using a *class*. No, not a class of students, but a class that represents a real object inside a program. You'll be learning about classes in this chapter.

The Object of Objects

A real-world *object,* such as the registration form used to register for a course, consists of attributes and behaviors (see Figure 2-1). An *attribute* is data associated with an object. The course name, course number, and your name and student number are examples of data associated with the registration form. A *behavior* is something performed by an object, such as processing, modifying, or canceling a course registration.

A programmer's job is to use an object-oriented programming language to translate attributes and behaviors of a real-world object into a class that consists of attributes and methods understood by a computer.

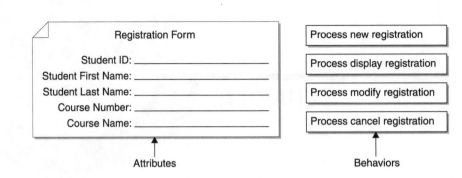

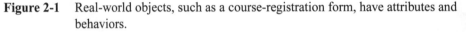

Figure 2-1   Real-world objects, such as a course-registration form, have attributes and behaviors.

NOTE: Method *and* function *are terms used to define a behavior in a program. Java programmers use the term* method, *and C++ programmers call it a* function. *Regardless of the name, a method and a function are used for the same purpose. Let's keep things simple when talking about behavior by using the term* method *throughout this book when referring to behavior, unless we are talking specifically about a C++ program.*

A Class

A *class* is a template that defines attributes and methods of a real-word object. Think of a class as a cookie cutter of the letter *A*. The cookie cutter isn't the letter *A* but rather defines what the letter *A* looks like. If you want a letter *A*, then place the cookie cutter on a cookie sheet of dough. If you want to make another letter *A*, you use the same cookie cutter and repeat the process. You can make as many letter *A*'s as you wish by using the cookie cutter.

The same is true about a class. When you want an object represented by the class, you create an *instance* of the class. An instance is the same as the letter *A* appearing on the cookie sheet of dough after you remove the cookie cutter.

Each instance contains the same attributes and methods that are defined in the class, although each instance has its own copy of those attributes. Instances use the same methods. Going a bit crackers with this explanation? Let's go to the cookie cutter to cut through the confusion. Remember that *instance* is another word for saying "a real cookie that is defined by the cookie cutter (class template)." Suppose the cookie cutter is in the shape of a dog. The dog's legs are of a particular width and length, as is the dog's tail. These are attributes of the dog. Each time the cookie cutter cuts into the dough, another dog cookie is created (instance). Say that you make two dog cookies this way. Each dog cookie (instance) has legs and a tail of the same width and length, but each has its own set (copy) of legs and a tail that is independent of other dog cookies.

A method is a behavior that is performed by a dog cookie. Okay, a dog cookie doesn't really do anything but sit quietly in your hand, so we'll have to use our imagination and pretend that the dog cookie can stand up on its legs only if you and you alone tell it how to stand up. The dog cookie ignores everyone else's instructions. Each dog cookie uses the same copy of the method (that is, your instructions) to perform the behavior of standing up on its legs.

Defining a Class

A class is defined in a class definition. A *class definition* defines attributes and methods that are members of the class. The form used to define a class is dependent on the programming language used to write the program. Here's a simple class definition using Java:

```
class RegistrationForm {
int studentNumber;
  int courseNumber;
}
```

And here's the same class definition using C++ (notice that a semicolon must follow the closing brace; otherwise, you'll receive a compiler error):

```
class RegistrationForm {
  int studentNumber;
  int courseNumber;
};
```

A class definition has three parts:

- Keyword class
- Class name
- Class body

The *keyword class* tells the compiler that you are defining a class. A keyword (also known as a *reserved word*) is a word that has special meaning to the programming language. The *class name* is a symbol given by the programmer that uniquely identifies a class from another class. The name of a class should relate to the real-world object that it is emulating, and the first letter of the name should be capitalized. In the previous example, the class name is `RegistrationForm` and represents a form used to register students for classes.

The *class body* is the portion of the class definition that is identified by open and close braces. Attributes and methods are defined within those braces. Two attributes are defined in this example—a student number and a course number. We'll include methods in the class later in this chapter.

Attributes

You probably remember from your programming course that a variable name is a reference to a memory location where you can store data. An *attribute* of a class is a variable called an *instance variable*. An instance variable references a memory address within the block of memory reserved for an instance. You can use an instance variable to store data in memory. It is called an instance variable because it is in the attribute portion of the class instance.

Memory is reserved by using a statement in a class definition that declares an instance variable. A *statement* is a computer instruction. Here is a declaration statement that declares two instance variables:

```
class RegistrationForm {
    int studentNumber;
    int courseNumber;
}
```

A variable and an instance variable are very similar, with a few exceptions. A variable is declared in a declaration statement within a program. Memory is reserved when the declaration statement executes. An instance variable is declared in a class definition. However, memory is reserved only when an instance is declared because a class definition is a template, and an instance is the computer's version of a real object.

Declaring an Instance Variable

An instance variable is declared within a class definition using a declaration statement. The form of a declaration is dependent on the programming language used to write the program. A declaration statement in Java or C++ consists of the following three parts, as illustrated in the class definitions shown earlier in this chapter:

- Data type
- Instance variable name
- Semicolon

Data Type

A *data type* is a keyword that tells the computer the kind of data you want to store in a memory location. The data type implies to the computer how much memory to reserve and how to handle the data stored once it is stored at that memory location.

Data types can baffle even professional programmers, so you're in good company if you are a little intimidated by the term *data type*. However, it is very important that you have a firm understanding of what a data type is and how to specify a data type when declaring a variable.

Think of a data type as the term "case of baseballs." You call the warehouse manager and say that you need to reserve enough space to hold one case of baseballs (see Figure 2-2). The warehouse manager knows how much space to reserve because he knows the size of a case of baseballs.

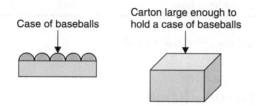

Case of baseballs

Carton large enough to hold a case of baseballs

Figure 2-2   A data type is similar to the term "a case of baseballs" because you and the warehouse manager know the size of a case of baseballs.

The same is true about a data type. You tell the computer to reserve space for an integer by using the data type `int`. The computer already knows how much memory to reserve to store an integer.

The data type also tells the computer the kind of data that will be stored at the memory location. This is important because computers manipulate data of some data types differently than data of other data types. This is similar to the warehouse manager who treats a case of fuel oil differently than a case of baseballs.

Here's another example: Suppose you want to store the number 1 in memory. You must decide whether the number 1 is an integer or a character. An integer can be used in arithmetic, whereas a character (such as the numbers in a house address) cannot be used in arithmetic until the character is converted to an integer. The data type tells the computer whether a number is an integer or a character. The computer then knows to use the appropriate steps to manipulate the data.

Each programming language has its own set of data types, commonly referred to as *primitive data types,* because they are basic data types. Table 2-1 contains primitive data types common to many programming languages.

Data Type	Range of Values
byte	−128 to 127
short	−32,768 to 32,767
int	−2,147,483,648 to 2,147,483,647

Table 2-1   Primitive Data Types

Data Type	Range of Values
long	−9,223,372,036,854,775,808 to 9,223,372,036,854,775,807
char	65,000 (Unicode)
float	3.4e−038 to 3.4e+038
double	1.7e−308 to 1.7e+308
boolean	true or false

Table 2-1   Primitive Data Types *(continued)*

Instance Variable Name

The name of an instance variable is a symbol given to that instance variable by a programmer, and it should represent the nature of the data stored at the memory location. For example, studentNumber is a perfect name for a variable used to store a student number because the name tells you the nature of the data associated with the variable. The variable name is used throughout the program to refer to the contents of the corresponding memory location.

The declaration statement must end with a semicolon in Java and C++. Otherwise, an error message is displayed when you try building the program.

Methods

Real-world objects have behaviors such as dropping a course, which you learned about in the previous chapter. A behavior is emulated in a program by a method that is associated with a class definition called a *member method*. Each instance of the class accesses a member method whenever the behavior needs to be performed in the program.

Think of a method as a group of statements that performs a specific behavior and is defined by specifying the following:

- Method name
- Method argument list
- Method body
- Return value

Programmers call this a *method definition*.

Method Name

A *method name* is a symbol a programmer gives to a method, much like how an instance variable name is a symbol used to refer to a location in memory. The name of the method should reflect the kind of behavior the method performs. For example, `dropCourse` is a good name for a method that drops a course from a student's schedule.

Argument List

Some methods don't require data from outside the method to perform a behavior. For example, a method that erases information entered into a registration form can do this with data already in the method definition.

Other methods require data from outside the method to perform a behavior. For example, the `dropCourse` method needs to know the course and the student who registered for the course in order to remove the course from the student's schedule. This data isn't included in the method definition but must be provided by part of the program that calls the method (see the "Calling a Method" section of this chapter).

An *argument list* is data outside the method definition that is needed by the method to perform a behavior. For example, the `dropCourse` method has an argument list containing the course number and the student number needed to remove the course from the student's schedule.

Data in an argument list is called an *argument,* and there can be one or multiple arguments in an argument list, depending on the nature of the behavior performed by the method.

An argument is declared by specifying a data type and a name for the argument. This is similar to declaring an instance variable, except the declaration is within parentheses and appears to the right of the method name, as shown here:

```
dropCourse(int courseNumber, int studentNumber)
```

This example contains two arguments: `int courseNumber` and `int studentNumber`. Collectively they are called an argument list. A comma must separate argument declarations. Once an argument is declared, the name of the argument is used in statements within the method definition to refer to data that is assigned to the argument when the method is called.

Method Body

The *method body* is part of a method that contains statements that are executed when the method is called. A method body is defined by open and close braces, called a *code block*. Statements are executed within the method body sequentially, beginning with the first statement and continuing until either a return statement is executed or the end of the method body is reached.

Defining a Method Within a Class Definition

A method definition is placed within the class definition, as shown in the following example. This method is called dropCourse and has two arguments—the course number and the student number. A value isn't returned by the dropCourse method, so the return value data type is void.

There aren't any statements in the method body because we don't want to clutter the example with unnecessary statements; instead, we included a comment showing you where statements belong:

```
class RegistrationForm {
  int studentNumber;
  int courseNumber;
   void dropCourse(int courseNumber, int studentNumber) {
     //Place statements for dropping a course here
   }
}
```

Return Value

Some methods do their thing and don't need to return any value to the statement that called them. This is the case with the method that erases information on a registration form because nothing needs to be returned.

Other methods are required to return data back to the part of the program that called them to give it the result. Data returned by a method is called a *return value*. For example, a method that calculates an expression, such as adding together two numbers, returns the result of the calculation as the return value.

Two steps are required in order to return a value. First, the data type of the return value must be specified to the left of the method name in the method definition. If a method does not return a value, then void is used as the data type, as shown here (the keyword void tells the computer that nothing is returned by the method):

```
void dropCourse(int courseNumber, int studentNumber)
```

However, let's suppose that the dropCourse() method returns true if it successfully drops the course and returns false if it is unable to drop the course. True and false are Boolean values. Therefore, the data type of the dropCourse() method must be changed to boolean, as shown here:

```
boolean dropCourse(int courseNumber, int studentNumber)
```

The second step is to use a return statement within the body of the method definition. The format of the return statement is dependent on the programming language used to write the program. In Java and C++, the return statement consists of three parts: the keyword `return`, the value to be returned, and a semicolon. The value can be the actual data, a variable, or an argument, as shown here:

```
return true;
return status;
```

The first return statement returns the Boolean value true. The second return statement returns a variable called `status`. Some place in the body of the method, the status variable is assigned a value of true or false, depending on whether or not the course is successfully dropped.

Combining a Class with a Program

Now that you know how to define a class and its attributes and methods, let's place a class definition in a program. A class definition is placed outside the main part of the program. We use the term *main* part because a program takes on a different form depending on what language is used to write the program.

The main part of a C++ program is the `main` function. A function is similar in concept to a method. The `main` function is the entry point into the program. The main part of a Java program is the `main` method of a class for applications, and it's the `Applet.init` method for applets.

A class definition must appear outside the `main` function in a C++ program and outside the Java application class definition in a Java program. We'll use a Java program called `MyJavaApplication` to illustrate where to place a class definition in a program.

The first part is the Java application class definition called `MyJavaApplication`, and the other part is the `RegistrationForm` class definition, which is defined in the previous section. Both are shown next.

The `RegistrationForm` class definition is placed outside of the `MyJavaApplication` class definition. Both are classes, each representing different things. The `MyJavaApplication` class represents the Java program, and the `RegistrationForm` class represents a registration form used to register students for class.

```
class MyJavaApplication {
public static void main (String args[]) {
     RegistrationForm regForm = new RegistrationForm();
     regForm.dropCourse(102,1234);
```

```
    }
}
class RegistrationForm {
    void dropCourse(int courseNumber, int studentNumber) {
    System.out.println("Course " + courseNumber + " has been
dropped from student " + studentNumber);
    }
}
```

Declaring an Instance of a Class

An instance of a class must be declared before attributes and methods of the class can be used in a program. That is, you must cut out a cookie in the dough using the cookie cutter before you can bake the cookie. The cookie cutter is the class definition, and the cookie cutout of the dough is an instance. Remember that a class definition (cookie cutter) only describes attributes and methods (that is, the legs and tail of the dog cookie) of the class.

Let's assume that a class definition has two attributes: studentNumber and courseNumber. In this example, both are integers that require 2 bytes of memory. Figure 2-3 shows how the instance of this class appears in memory. The class definition doesn't reserve any memory but simply defines what memory must be reserved when an instance is created.

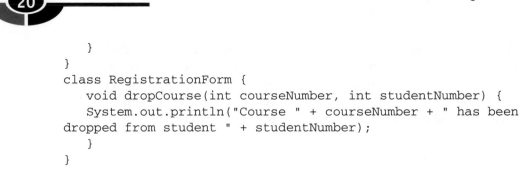

Figure 2-3   This figure shows how an instance of the `RegistrationForm` class reserves memory.

An instance of a class is created in a declaration statement, as shown in this Java example:

```
RegistrationForm myRegistrationForm = new RegistrationForm();
```

This statement looks imposing, so let's take apart the statement and see how it works. We'll begin with the right side of the assignment operator:

```
new RegistrationForm()
```

This tells the computer to dynamically reserve a block of memory the size of the `RegistrationForm` class. *Dynamically* means that memory is reserved when the computer executes the program, which is called runtime. Memory for most variables and arrays is reserved at compile time, using the following declaration statement:

```
int grade;
```

The *class size* is the size of all the class's attributes. Reserving memory dynamically occurs when the program executes rather than when the program is compiled.

Once the computer reserves the block of memory, it returns a pointer to the first memory address of the block. A *pointer* is like someone pointing to your instructor's office.

Let's move on to the second part of the statement:

```
RegistrationForm myRegistrationForm
```

This portion of the statement declares a reference to an instance of the `RegistrationForm` class called `myRegistrationForm`. This is a mouthful to say, so let dissect it to get a better understanding at what it means.

A *reference* is something that refers you to something else. In this case, the reference is going to refer you to an instance of the `RegistrationForm` class.

The name of the reference in the previous example is `myRegistrationForm`. This is like saying `myRootCanalSpecialist`. You use the name of the reference whenever you want to refer to the instance of `RegistrationForm`.

A reference is not an instance of a class. It is only a symbol that refers to an instance. The final part of the declaration statement assigns the pointer to the instance to the reference using the assignment operator. You then use the reference (`myRegistrationForm`) in the program whenever you want to refer to the instance of the class.

Initializing an Instance Variable

Initialization is the process of assigning a value to a variable when the variable is declared. Programmers do this to prevent a possible error if the variable is used without being assigned a value. Think of this as telling the computer to give you what is in a carton, but you've never stored anything in the carton, so the computer complains.

As you probably remember from your programming course, a variable is initialized by assigning a value to the variable when it is declared, such as in the following statement:

```
String status = "No Change";
```

In C++, an instance variable cannot be initialized this way, but in Java it can. For C++, an instance variable must be initialized using a special member method called a *constructor* that's automatically called when an instance of a class is declared. The constructor has the same name as the class. Constructors exist in both C++ and Java, as well as in other OOP languages.

How to define a constructor to initialize an instance variable is shown next. This listing defines the RegistrationForm class that you learned about. The RegistrationForm class declares an attribute called status and defines two methods. The first method is RegistrationForm, which is the constructor because it has the same name as the class. The other method is dropCourse, which you saw earlier.

The constructor assigns the message Course Not Changed to the instance variable status. This is the default status for each instance of the class. The value of the status instance variable is changed from the default value to the message Course Dropped by the dropCourse method.

```
class MyJavaApplication {
    public static void main (String args[]) {
        RegistrationForm regForm = new RegistrationForm();
        regForm.dropCourse(CS102,1234);
        System.out.println("Status: " + regForm.status);
    }
}
class RegistrationForm {
    String status;

    void RegistrationForm () {
        status = "Course Not Changed.";
    }
    void dropCourse(int courseNumber, int studentNumber)
{status = "Course: "+ courseNumber + " is dropped for
student: " + studentNumber;
    }
}
```

Accessing an Instance Variable

An instance variable is accessed in a program basically the same way you call a method member. First, create an instance of the class and then use the name of the instance and the dot operator to reference the instance variable. Here's how to access the status instance variable from within your program:

```
instanceName.instanceVariableName
```

An instance of the RegistrationForm class, called regForm, is declared in the main method. Next, the dropCourse method is called as described in the "Calling a Method" section of this chapter. After the dropCourse method executes, the value of the status instance value is printed on the screen by directly accessing the instance variable.

Assigning a Value to an Instance Variable from Your Program

The value of an instance variable can be changed using an assignment statement in your program. This process is nearly identical to how a value is assigned to a variable, except that you use the name of the instance to reference the instance variable, as shown here:

```
regForm.status = "No Status";
```

Any change in the value of the instance variable is accessible to the member methods. How this is done is shown below. After an instance of the RegistrationForm class is declared in the main method, an assignment statement changes the default value of the instance variable status to the message No Status.

The next statement calls the displayStatus method that is defined in the RegistrationForm class. This method displays the value of the status instance variable on the screen. The message No Status appears when this method is called.

The dropCourse method then changes the value of the status instance variable to Course Dropped, which is then displayed by the program.

CAUTION: *Many programmers frown on letting a program directly change the value of an instance value because this practice is fraught with the danger that the data will be corrupted. Programmers prefer that only member methods change an instance variable's value. That way, safeguards can be placed in the member method to prevent data from being corrupted. A program then calls the member method whenever it needs to change the value of an instance variable.*

```
class MyJavaApplication {
   public static void main (String args[]) {
      RegistrationForm regForm = new RegistrationForm();
      regForm.status = "No Status";
      regForm.displayStatus();
      regForm.dropCourse(CS102,1234);
      System.out.println("Status: " + regForm.status);
   }
}
```

```
class RegistrationForm {
   String status;
   void RegistrationForm () {
     status = "Course Not Changed.";
   }
  void dropCourse(int courseNumber, int studentNumber) {
    status = "Course: "+ courseNumber + " is dropped for
student: " + studentNumber;

  }
  void displayStatus();
     System.out.println("Status: " + status);
  }
}
```

Calling a Method

Before you can call a member method, you must declare an instance of the class, unless the method being called is a static method. A static method is a method that is not associated with a class, which you'll learn about in Chapter 4. As you'll remember, creating an instance makes a real copy of the attributes and methods of the class. The instance is then used to call the method.

Let's see how this works in the preceding listing. The first statement in the `main` method declares an instance of the `RegistrationForm` class. The instance is called `regForm`.

Once the instance is declared, the name of the instance is used to call the `dropCourse` method, which is defined in the `RegistrationForm` class. The method is called by using the following items:

- The name of the instance
- The dot operator
- The name of the method

The *dot operator* is a period that says, "The method to my right is a member of the instance to my left and is used to reference attributes and methods of an instance of a class."

Passing Parameters

If a method has an argument list, then data must be included between the parentheses when the method is called. This is called *passing a parameter.* Data placed between the parentheses is called a *parameter list.* Each data element on the parameter list is called a *parameter,* and a comma must separate each parameter.

Most programmers treat parameters and arguments synonymously.

The `dropCourse` method requires two parameters because its method definition defines two arguments in its argument list. This means that we must pass two parameters when calling the `dropCourse` method. Each parameter must match the corresponding argument in the argument list.

Think of parameters in a parameter list and arguments in an argument list stacked on top of each other, as shown here. A parameter must be in the same order as its corresponding argument and must be of a compatible data type to the corresponding argument data type:

```
dropCourse(102, 1234);
void dropCourse(int courseNumber, int studentNumber) {
```

Values of the parameters are copied to arguments in the argument list. This is referred to as *passing by value.* Values in the parameter list appear in two locations in memory—one location for the copy in the parameter list, and another location for the copy in the argument list.

The names of arguments are used in statements within the method to access values stored in arguments. In the previous listing (in the section "Assigning a Value to an Instance Variable from Your Program") names of arguments are used in a statement that prints the value of each argument on the screen.

Using a Return Value

The part of the program that calls a method accesses a return value by using an assignment operator placed to the left of the call to the method. As you'll probably recall from your programming course, an assignment operator copies the value on the right of the assignment operator to the variable or expression on the left of the assignment operator.

Let's see how this works. The next listing defines a class called `RegistrationForm` that contains the dropCourse() member method, which is used to drop a course, and returns a Boolean value as the return value.

An instance of the `RegistrationForm` class called regForm is declared in the second statement within the main method and is used to call the `add` method, passing it two parameters. Notice that two things happen in the statement that calls the dropCourse() method.

First, the dropCourse() method is called. Then, once the dropCourse() method has finishing doing its thing, the value returned by the dropCourse() method is assigned to the variable result using the assignment operator. The result variable is then used in the conditional expression in the `if` statement. A message reporting the results of the dropCourse() method is then displayed on the screen.

```java
class MyJavaApplication {
public static void main (String args[]) {
        RegistrationForm regForm = new RegistrationForm();
        boolean result;
        result = regForm.dropCourse(102,1234);
        if (result)
            System.out.println("Course dropped.");
        else
            System.out.println("Unable to drop the course.");
    }
}
class RegistrationForm {
    boolean dropCourse(int courseNumber, int studentNumber) {
        return true;
    }
}
```

Quiz

1. What is an instance variable?

2. How do you determine the size of a class?

3. Explain the steps necessary to create an instance of a class.

4. How do you declare an instance variable?

5. What is a data type?

6. Explain the parts of a method definition.

7. What is the difference between an argument list and a parameter list?

8. Explain the steps for calling a member method.

9. What is a constructor and how do you define one?

10. How do you access an instance variable from within your program?

3

Encapsulation

Encapsulation is one of those computer terms that has an overtone of sci-fi and rocket science combined, and yet you use encapsulation every day of your life. Do you have your credit cards, money, and your driver's licenses in your wallet? Do you have pens, paper, textbook, and your laptop in a bag that you take to school? If so, then you use encapsulation. Encapsulation is putting related things together to form a new object. It may seem trivial, but you'll learn in this chapter that encapsulation has revolutionized the way programs are written and has become a cornerstone of object-oriented programming.

Parts of a Program Come Together

For a long time, programmers used procedural programming languages such as C to group together instructions into one task, called a *procedure*. A procedure is the same as a function in C and C++ and a method in Java.

Think of a procedure as the definition of an object's behavior. For example, there is a procedure for a student to register for a course. The student is the object and the procedure, to register for a course, is a behavior performed by a student. Attributes of a student, such as student ID, are used to carry out the procedure.

In the real world, objects and their behaviors and attributes are grouped together. For example, you can't register for a course if you are not a student. Steps are taken to prevent someone who is not a student from receiving a student ID and from submitting a course registration. This is because attributes of a student and behaviors of a student are grouped together and associated with a student. If you are not a student, then you cannot perform the behaviors of a student.

However, in the world of procedural programming, procedures and attributes are not grouped together and associated with an object. This means a programmer could call the registration procedure to register a person who is not a student.

The following example illustrates this problem. This is a C/C++ program that defines a function (procedure) called `registration`. The `registration()` function receives a student ID and course number in its argument list and displays those values in a message on the screen. As you'll recall from your programming classes, an argument list contains information needed for the procedure to carry out its task.

Two variables (attributes) are declared in the `main()` function. These are `studentID` and `courseNumber`. Each is initialized with a value, which is passed to the `registration()` function in the next statement.

Notice that there is no association between variables and the `registration()` method, except that variable names and the name of the function imply they have something to do with a student:

```
#include <string>
#include <iostream>
using namespace std;
void registration(string studentID, string courseNumber)
{
    cout << "Registration Accepted: " + studentID + " "
        + courseNumber << endl;
}
int main()
{
    string studentID = "12345", courseNumber = "9876";
    registration(studentID, courseNumber);
    return 0;
}
```

The lack of an association between attributes and a procedure is a drawback of procedural programming languages. This is of little concern when one programmer develops an entire application because the programmer knows not to pass the `registration()` function a variable containing a nonstudent. It becomes troublesome when a team of programmers designs the application because each programmer on the team must remember to pass the `registration()` function only student information.

Here's the problem: There is no way in a procedural programming language to force an association between attributes and procedures, which can lead to inadvertent misuse of the association by the programming team.

Here's the solution: Write the program using an object-oriented programming language such as C++ or Java. An object-oriented programming language enables a programmer to encapsulate attributes and procedures and associate them with an object. This greatly reduces the misuse to attributes and procedures.

The solution came with the introduction of object-oriented programming in the 1980s. Object-oriented programming uses an object-oriented programming language such as C++ or Java to mimic real-world objects in a program by defining a class.

What Is Encapsulation?

Encapsulation is a technique of linking together attributes and procedures to form an object. The only way to access attributes and procedures of an object is to create an instance of the object.

As you'll recall from Chapter 2, you create an object within a program by defining a class. The class definition contains the definitions of attributes and procedures (functions in C++ and methods in Java).

Figure 3-1 shows a diagram of a class that defines the object Student. The top of the diagram is the list of attributes that describe a student. These are a student's ID, student name, and whether or not the student graduated. The bottom of the diagram is a list of procedures associated with a student. These write and display information

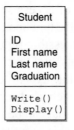

Figure 3-1   A class diagram showing attributes and procedures that are encapsulated in the `Student` class definition.

about a student. The attributes and procedures described in Figure 3-1 are said to be *encapsulated* in the Student class.

Why Use Encapsulation?

Some programmers may think encapsulation is simply a clever way to make your program orderly by putting related attributes and procedures under one roof. Although this is true, protection is the reason for encapsulation.

Previously you learned in this chapter that there is really no protection against the improper use of attributes and procedures in procedural programming. Both are available for a programmer to use without any checks and balances.

You might say that encapsulation enables a programmer to institute those checks and balances by placing attributes and procedures in a class and then defining rules in the class to control its access.

Protection Using Access Specifiers

A programmer controls access to attributes and procedures of a class by using access specifiers within a class definition. An *access specifier* is a keyword of a programming language that tells the computer what part of the program can access attributes and procedures that are members of a class.

Think of access specifiers as cafeterias. There is the students' cafeteria, the teachers' cafeteria, and a luncheonette. Each is an access specifier. Only students can use the facilities (attributes and procedures) of the students' cafeteria. Only teachers can use the facilities of the teachers' cafeteria. However, on occasion, a friend of a teacher is permitted to eat lunch in the teachers' cafeteria, and anyone can use the facilities of the luncheonette.

Java and C++ have three kinds of access specifiers—public, private, and protected. The *public access* specifier (the luncheonette, in this example) determines attributes and procedures that are accessible by using an instance of the class. The *private access* specifier (the students' and teachers' cafeterias) identifies attributes and procedures that are only accessible by a procedure that is a defined by the class. The *protected access* specifier (a teacher's friend eating at the teachers' cafeteria) stipulates attributes and procedures that can be inherited and used by another class. More on inheritance a little later in this chapter.

Public Access Specifier

When you declare an instance of a class (see Chapter 2), you can use the instance to access attributes and procedures that are defined in the public access specifier section of the class. You define the public access specifier section of the class by using the keyword `public`, as shown in the following example.

This example is written in C++ and requires that a colon follow the keyword `public` and that public attributes and procedures be defined beneath the `public` keyword. As you'll see in the "Encapsulation in Action Using Java" section of this chapter, Java requires that the keyword `public` be used at the beginning of each definition of public attributes and procedures.

One procedure defined in this example is placed beneath the public access specifier. This means the procedure can be called directly from within the program by declaring an instance of the `Student` class. Here's the example:

```cpp
class Student
{
    public:
        void Display(){
            //Place statements here
        }
};
```

You can access directly the attributes and procedures defined using the keyword `public` within the program by using the name of the instance, the dot operator, and the name of the attribute or procedure being accessed.

Let's say that you want to display student information from within a program. Here's what you need to do:

```cpp
#include <iostream>
using namespace std;
class Student
{
    public:
        void Display(){
            cout << "Statements go here." << endl;
        }
};
int main() {
    Student myStudent;
    myStudent.Display();
return 0;
}
```

The first statement in the main() function declares an instance of the Student class. The second statement calls the Display() procedure of the Student class.

Private Access Specifier

The private access specifier restricts access to attributes and procedures for procedures that are members of the same class. The next example illustrates how this is done. The goal is to prevent the student ID, student name, and graduation status attributes from being used directly by the instance of the Student class. This is accomplished by using the private access specifier.

The private access specifier does not prevent the Display() procedure from accessing these attributes because the Display() procedure is a member of the Student class. Notice that you don't need to create an instance of the Student class to use other members (attributes and procedures) within the procedures of the class.

```
#include <iostream>
using namespace std;
class Student
{
   public:
      void Display(){
         cout << "Student: " << m_ID << " " << m_First << " " <<
         m_Last << "
Graduated: " << m_Graduation << endl;
      }
   private:
      int m_ID, m_Graduation;
      char m_First[16], m_Last[16];
 };
int main() {
   Student myStudent;
   myStudent.Display();
return 0;
}
```

The technique shown in the previous example is a cornerstone of object-oriented programming because it requires that other programmers use a member procedure to access attributes of the class. This enables the programmer who created the class to encode rules in member procedures that govern how attributes are to be used.

Suppose you were a programmer who wanted to display student information. You couldn't access student information directly. Instead, you must call a procedure member of the class to display student information. This gives the programmer who defined the class total control over what attributes are accessed and how they are displayed.

Protected Access Specifier

The protected access specifier identifies the attributes and procedures that can be used only by procedures that are members of the class and by procedures that are members of a class that inherits the class.

The class being inherited is called the *super class* (Java) or the *base class* (C++), and the class that inherits another class is called the *subclass* (Java) or the *derived class* (C++).

Inheritance is covered in Chapter 5, but we'll give you a sneak preview here and throughout this chapter so you'll be able to understand how the protected access specifier works. Let's say that there are two classes. One class is called Student and the other GradStudent.

The Student class contains attributes and behaviors that are characteristic of all students. The GradStudent class contains attributes and behaviors that are unique to graduate students (see Figure 3-2), which include the attributes and behaviors of all students. A graduate student is, after all, a student.

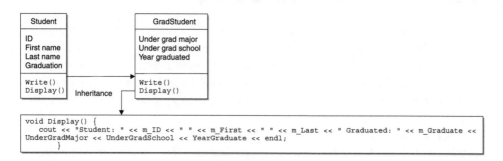

Figure 3-2   The GradStudent class has attributes and procedures that are the same and some that are different from the Student class.

Rather than duplicate the attributes and behaviors of the Student class in the GradStudent class, we can use an object-oriented programming language to have the GradStudent class inherit all or some of the attributes and behaviors of the Student class.

Attributes and behaviors defined using the public access specifier and the protected access specifier can be directly used by the GradStudent class. The following C++ example shows how to use the protected access specifier:

```
#include <iostream>
using namespace std;
class Student
{
```

```
    public:
        void Display(){
            cout << "Student: " << m_ID << " " << m_First << " "
            << m_Last << "
Graduated: " << m_Graduation << endl;
        }
    protected:
        int m_ID, m_Graduation;
        char m_First[16], m_Last[16];
 };
int main() {
    Student myStudent;
    myStudent.Display();
return 0;
```

Encapsulation in Action Using C++

Let's take a look at how the public and private access specifiers are used in a C++ program. The following example defines a class called Student whose attributes are a student ID, student name, and the student's graduation status. Two member functions are defined in the Student class. (We'll use the term *member function* in place of the term *procedure* in this section because a procedure in C++ is called a function.)

Functions associated with a class are called *member functions*. The first member function is Write(), and it assigns values to attributes. The other member function is Display(), which displays values stored in attributes. This is the same Display() member function you learned about in the previous section. Neither member functions return a value.

We want attributes of the Student class to be accessed only through the Write() and Display() functions and not directly within the program by using an instance of the Student class. That is, the only way to store a value in an attribute or to display attributes is by calling a member function of the Student class.

To make this happen, we'll need to place the definition of the Write() and Display() functions beneath the public access specifier and then place attributes below the private access specifier.

NOTE: *In the real world, class definitions are typically contained in a class library that is made accessible to a program during the linking process. The programmer doesn't have direct access to the class definition. Instead, the programmer is provided with documentation of public and protected attributes and member functions, when available, of the class definition. In this example, the programmer would receive documentation on how to use the* Write() *member function and the* Display() *member function of the* Student *class. The programmer would not know anything about the attributes of the* Student *class because the attributes are in the private access specifier and cannot be directly accessed by the programmer from within the program. In the real world, the class documentation mentions private members to help a programmer understand how the public function accesses them.*

Inside the Write() Member Function

You'll remember from Figure 3-1 that the Student class has two behaviors that are encoded in the form of the Write() member function and the Display() member function. The Write() member function writes values to attributes of the class, and the Display() member function displays those attributes.

The Write() member function has four arguments in its argument list, as shown here:

```
Write(int ID, int Grad, char Fname[], char Lname[])
```

The first two arguments are integers representing the student ID and an indicator of whether the student has graduated. The other two arguments are character arrays that represent the first name and last name of the student.

Notice that these arrays don't have a definitive size, as indicated by the empty brackets. As you'll recall from your C++ programming class, the size of these arrays is set when the student's first and last names are received by the member function. The size then becomes the same size as the student's first and last name.

The body of the definition of the Write() member function assigns values of the argument list to attributes. An assignment statement is used to assign values to integer attributes. The strcpy() function is called to assign the values of the Fname and Lname character arrays, which are strings, to the corresponding attributes.

Inside the Display() Member Function

The Display() member function, shown here, reads values of attributes and displays each of them on the screen. A series of insertion operators (<<) form a cascade of strings and attributes to create the text that is shown. (Refer to *C++ Demystified*, also by McGraw-Hill/Osborne, to brush up on your C++ programming terms.)

```
void Display(){
    cout << "Student: " << m_ID << " " << m_First << " " << m_Last << "
        Graduated:
" << m_Graduation << endl;
}
```

Names of attributes are dispersed throughout string literals. String literals are labels for the attributes when they are displayed. The insertion operator sends the output to the instance of cout, which references standard out. Standard out is typically the screen.

Inside the main() Function

An instance of the Student class called myStudent is declared in the first statement of the main() function. You'll recall from your C++ programming course that the main() function is the entry point into a C++ program.

The second statement uses the name of the instance to call the Write() member function. The parameter list of the Write() member function consists of the student's ID, an integer indicating whether or not the student has graduated, and the student's first name and last name. We'll use 1 to indicate that the student has graduated and 0 to indicate that the student hasn't graduated yet.

The last statement in the main() function uses the name of the instance to call the Display() member function, which displays the value of attributes on the screen.

A compiler error occurs if the programmer attempts to directly access attributes of the Student class because attributes are within the private access specifier section of the class definition.

```
#include <string>
#include <iostream>
using namespace std;
class Student
{
    public:
        void Write(int ID, int Grad, char Fname[], char Lname[]) {
```

```
            m_ID = ID;
            m_Graduation = Grad;
            strcpy(m_First,Fname);
            strcpy(m_Last, Lname);
        }
        void Display(){
            cout << "Student: " << m_ID << " " << m_First << " "
                << m_Last << " Graduated: " << m_Graduation << endl;
        }
    private:
        int m_ID, m_Graduation;
        char m_First[16], m_Last[16];
};
void main()
{
    Student myStudent;
    myStudent.Write(10, 1,"Bob","Smith");
    myStudent.Display();
}
```

If you use an instance to access a private or protected member of a class, you'll experience a compiler error. In the last statement of the next example, the program tries to access the m_ID member of the Student class. The m_ID member is a private member and can only be accessed by a member function of the Student class.

You'll receive the following error message if you try to compile this example:

```
'm_ID' : cannot access private member declared in class 'Student'
#include <string>
#include <iostream>
using namespace std;
class Student
{
    public:
        void Write(int ID, int Grad, char Fname[], char Lname[]) {
            m_ID = ID;
            m_Graduation = Grad;
            strcpy(m_First,Fname);
            strcpy(m_Last, Lname);
        }
        void Display(){
            cout << "Student: " << m_ID << " " << m_First << " " << m_Last
                << " Graduated: " << m_Graduation << endl;
        }
    private:
```

```
        int m_ID, m_Graduation;
        char m_First[16], m_Last[16];
};
void main()
{
    Student myStudent;
    myStudent.Write(10, 1,"Bob","Smith");
    myStudent.Display();
    myStudent.m_ID = 2;
}
```

Protected Access Specifier in Action

You learned previously in this chapter that a class can inherit attributes and procedures of another class that are defined within the public access specifier or protected access specifier of the class. You'll learn all the nitty-gritty about inheritance in Chapter 5, but let's take a glimpse of what's to come by reviewing an example of the protected access specifier.

The following example defines two classes: Student and GradStudent. The Student class defines attributes and procedures of any student, which you saw in the previous example. The GradStudent class defines attributes and procedures of a graduate student. A graduate student is a student; therefore, a graduate student has the attributes and procedures of a student. In addition, a graduate student has attributes and procedures that are unique to only a graduate student.

This is a perfect situation to have the GradStudent class inherit the Student class. In C++, you indicate that a class inherits from another class by placing a colon and the name of the inherited class in the class definition, as shown in this example. Notice that a colon and the name of the Student class follow the GradStudent class name. This tells the computer that the GradStudent class inherits the Student class.

Also notice that attributes of the Student class are placed in the protected access specifier section of the Student class definition. This makes the attributes available to member functions defined in the Student class and member functions defined in the GradStudent class, but those attributes cannot be directly accessed by other parts of the program.

```
#include <string>
#include <iostream>
using namespace std;
class Student
{
```

```cpp
    public:
        void Write(int ID, int Grad, char Fname[], char Lname[]) {
            m_ID = ID;
            m_Graduation = Grad;
            strcpy(m_First,Fname);
            strcpy(m_Last, Lname);
        }
        void Display(){
            cout << "Student: " << m_ID << " " << m_First << " " << m_Last
                << " Graduated: " << m_Graduation << endl;
        }
    protected:
        int m_ID, m_Graduation;
        char m_First[16], m_Last[16];
    };
class GradStudent : Student
{
    public:
        void Write(int ID, int Grad, char Fname[], char Lname[], int yrGrad,
            char unSch[], char major[]) {
            m_ID = ID;
            m_Graduation = Grad;
            YearGraduated = yrGrad;
            strcpy(m_First,Fname);
            strcpy(m_Last, Lname);
            strcpy(m_UndergradSchool,unSch);
            strcpy(m_Major, major);
         }
        void Display(){
            cout << "Student: " << m_ID << " " << m_First << " " << m_Last
                << " Graduated: " << m_Graduation << " " << m_UndergradSchool
                << " " << m_Major << " " << YearGraduated<< endl;
        }
    private:
        int YearGraduated;
        char m_UndergradSchool[80];
        char m_Major[80];
};
void main()
{
    GradStudent myStudent;
    myStudent.Write(10, 1,"Bob","Smith", 2000,"Columbia University", "CS");
    myStudent.Display();
}
```

Inside the GradStudent Class

The GradStudent class definition defines its own versions of the Write() member function and the Display() member function. We use the term *member function* instead of *procedure* because this example is written in C++, where procedures are called *functions* and functions defined in a class are called *member functions*.

There is a practical reason for having to redefine these member functions. The Write() member function and the Display() member function of the Student class cannot write values to or display attributes of the GradStudent class. The redefined member functions in the GradStudent class write values to attributes and display attributes defined both in the Student class and in the GradStudent class.

Notice that the redefined member functions use attributes defined in the Student class as if it was defined in the GradStudent class. This is made possible because the GradStudent class inherits attributes defined in the protected access specifier section of the Student class.

The GradStudent class defines its own attributes that are placed in the private access specifier section of the class. Only member functions defined in the GradStudent class can access these attributes. The Student class does not have access to member functions and attributes defined in the GradStudent class. You'll learn the reason for this in Chapter 5.

The attributes defined in the GradStudent class are used to store the year that the student was awarded an undergraduate degree. Other attributes are used to store the name of the school that awarded the degree and the student's undergraduate major.

The main function in this example is nearly identical to the main function of the previous example with two exceptions. First, an instance of the GradStudent class is declared rather than an instance of the Student class because the program is focused on a graduate student rather than any kind of student. The other exception is that the program calls member functions of the GradStudent class.

How does the computer know to use the Write() and Display() member functions defined in the GradStudent class and not those defined in the Student class?

The answer: By default, the computer uses a member function defined in the GradStudent class whenever there is a conflict with a member function named in the Student class.

Encapsulation in Action Using Java

Encapsulation is used in a Java program nearly the same way as it is used in a C++ program, except different syntax applies. Let's take a look at how encapsulation works in Java. The next example is the Java version of the C++ program that illustrates the private access specifier.

Two classes are defined in this example. The first class is StudentInfo, which is the Java application class. As you'll recall from your Java application course, a Java application is contained within a class definition called the Java application class. The Java application class is the entry point to a Java application.

The other class definition is Student. The Student class is the class that defines attributes and methods of a student and has the same purpose as the Student class in the previous C++ examples. We'll use the term *method* instead of *procedure* in this section because a procedure in Java is called a method.

Let's begin our exploration with the definition of the Student class. You'll need to understand how the Student class works before you can understand how the class is used in the Java application class.

Notice that the Student class resembles the Student class defined in the C++ example. Both class definitions define the same two methods and the same four attributes. These methods also perform the same functionality as methods defined in the Student class of the C++ example.

However, there are three subtle differences in the Java version. Notice that the class definition doesn't have a public access specifier section and a private access specifier section. Instead, the keywords public and private precede the name of the attribute and method to perform the same functionality as the public access specifier section and private access specifier section in the C++ version of this program.

Another difference is that the String data type is used instead of a char array for the student's name. The last difference is the way text is displayed on the screen in the Display() member method. In Java, the System.out.print() method is used to display text on the screen. The System.out.print() method displays text without a carriage return and line feed at the end of the line. We do this because the Display() member method of the GradStudent class definition displays text on the same line as the Display member method of the Student class. You'll see how this is done in the next example:

```
class StudentInfo {
    public static void main (String args[]) {
        Student myStudent = new Student();
```

```
        myStudent.Write(10, 1,"Bob","Smith");
        myStudent.Display();
    }
}
class Student
{
    public void Write(int ID, int Grad, String Fname, String Lname) {
        m_ID = ID;
        m_Graduation = Grad;
        m_First = Fname;
        m_Last = Lname;
     }
    public void Display(){
        System.out.println( "Student: " + m_ID + " " + m_First + " " +
            m_Last + " Graduated: " + m_Graduation);
    }
    private int m_ID, m_Graduation;
    private String m_First;
    private String m_Last;
}
```

Protected Access Specifier in Action

The protected keyword is used in a Java class definition to tell the computer that another class can inherit an attribute or member method. This is nearly identical to the protected access specifier used in the C++ example.

The following is the Java application version of the C++ example that defines a Student class and a GradStudent class, shown previously in this chapter. As you probably suspect, there are subtle differences between the two programs. We'll explore those differences here.

The following example declares three classes. The first two class definitions are the same as in the example of the private access specifier. The third class definition is new. It is the definition of a graduate student and is called GradStudent. The GradStudent class inherits attributes and member methods of the Student class by using the keyword extends followed by the name of the class it inherits, which is Student in this example.

The Student class definition is nearly the same as the Student class definition used in the private access specifier example, with one exception. Notice that attributes are preceded with the keyword protected, which tells the computer that attributes can be accessed by member methods of the GradStudent class. The GradStudent class definition is the same as the GradStudent class definition in the C++ example.

An instance of the GradStudent class is declared in the main() method of the Java application class definition and is then used to call the Write() method to assign values to attributes of the GradStudent class and attributes inherited from the Student class. Those values are then displayed on the screen by calling the Display() method of the GradStudent class.

Notice that the Display() method of the GradStudent class is slightly different from the Display() method of the Student class. This looks a little confusing, so let's take a closer look, beginning with the Display() method of the Student class.

The Display() method of the Student class displays values of attributes defined in the Student class. The Display() method of the GradStudent class enhances the capability of the Display() method of the Student class by displaying both attributes of the Student class and attributes of the GradStudent class. Here's how this is done: Remember that the GradStudent class inherits public and protected members of the Student class. This means that the Display() method of the GradStudent class can call the Display() method of the Student class, which it does in this example. A class that is being inherited is called a *super class*, and the keyword super is used to access its attributes and member methods.

In this example, super.Display() tells the computer to call the Display() method of the Student class, which displays attributes of the Student class on the screen. The next statement displays attributes of the GradStudent class on the same lines as attributes of the Student class.

```
class StudentInfo {
    public static void main (String args[]) {
        GradStudent myStudent = new GradStudent();
        myStudent.Write(10, 1,"Bob","Smith", 2000,"Columbia University",
            "CS");
        myStudent.gradDisplay();
    }
}
class Student
{
    public void Write(int ID, int Grad, String Fname, String Lname) {
        m_ID = ID;
        m_Graduation = Grad;
        m_First = Fname;
        m_Last = Lname;
    }
    public void Display(){
        System.out.print( "Student: " + m_ID + " " + m_First + " " +
            m_Last + " Graduated: " + m_Graduation);
```

```
    }
    protected int m_ID, m_Graduation;
    protected String m_First;
    protected String m_Last;
}
class GradStudent extends Student
{
    public void Write(int ID, int Grad, String Fname, String Lname, int
        yrGrad, String unSch, String major) {
        m_ID = ID;
        m_Graduation = Grad;
        YearGraduated = yrGrad;
        m_First = Fname;
        m_Last = Lname;
        m_UndergradSchool = unSch;
        m_Major = major;
    }
    public void Display(){
        super.Display();
        System.out.println( " " + m_UndergradSchool + " " + m_Major +
            " " + YearGraduated);
    }
    int YearGraduated;
    private String m_UndergradSchool;
    private String m_Major;
};
```

Quiz

1. What is encapsulation?

2. What is the benefit of using encapsulation?

3. What is an access specifier?

4. What is a public access specifier?

5. What is a private access specifier?

6. What is a protected access specifier?

7. What portions of a super class can be used by a subclass?

8. How are access specifiers used differently in Java and C++?

9. Can a super class access portions of a subclass?

10. Why do programmers require that some attributes of a class be accessed only by a member procedure?

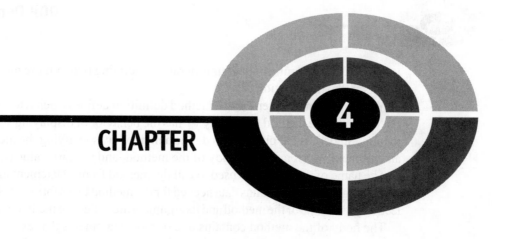

CHAPTER

Methods and Polymorphism

Polymorphism sounds like a disease old people are tested for every year. However, you probably surmise that polymorphism has something to do with object-oriented programming rather than medicine. *Polymorphism* means that something has the ability to appear in many shapes—and that something is a method of an object-oriented programming language. In this case, a shape is the behavior that method performs. In this chapter, you'll learn about polymorphism and how to use it in an object-oriented program.

Methods

Let's begin our trek into the world of polymorphism with a look back at methods. You might wonder why we begin with a review of methods. We do so because you

implement polymorphism in your program by defining two or more methods (more on this in the next section).

You learned in Chapter 2 that a method definition defines a behavior of an object. For example, the method `Display()` has the behavior of displaying student information. Student is the object. You define a method by specifying the method name, an argument list (if any), the body of the method, and a return value (if any).

The name of the method is used to call the method from a statement in a program, and the argument list contains data needed for the method to perform its behavior. Collectively, the name of the method and its argument are called the method's *signature*.

The body of the method contains one or more statements that execute when the method is called. This is where the behavior is actually performed. The return value is the value returned to the program after the method finishes completing its behavior. Some methods don't require an argument list or return value.

Polymorphism

Polymorphism technically means that one thing has the ability to take many shapes, as you learned in the introduction to this chapter. In programming terms, the "thing" is the name of a method and the "shape" is the behavior performed by the method. Therefore, polymorphism in programming terms means that the name of a method can have many behaviors.

Confused? Then you're in good company. The concept of polymorphism confuses many programmers, but the confusion usually goes away as soon as you see an example of polymorphism in action.

A real-world example of polymorphism is an on/off switch. Everyone is familiar with the concept of an on/off switch, what it does, and how to operate one. They realize that to start or activate something, you turn it on, and to stop or deactivate it, you turn it off. In other words, it works as a sort of "toggle." However, the reality is that, internally, the on/of switch for your house lights is dramatically different from the on/off switch for your computer. Polymorphism in this case involves two same-named items (on/off switches) performing the same task (turning something on or off), despite being very different internally.

Let's return to the StudentInfo Java application from Chapter 3 and modify it to illustrate polymorphism. As you'll recall, the application defines two classes: the `Student` class and the `GradStudent` class, as shown here:

```
class Student
{
    public void Write(int ID, int Grad, String Fname, String Lname) {
        m_ID = ID;
        m_Graduation = Grad;
```

```
      m_First = Fname;
      m_Last = Lname;
   }
   public void Display(){
      System.out.println( "Student: " + m_ID + " " + m_First + " " +
        m_Last + " Graduated: " + m_Graduation);
   }
   private int m_ID, m_Graduation;
   private String m_First;
   private String m_Last;
}

class GradStudent extends Student
{
   public void Write(int ID, int Grad, String Fname, String Lname,
int yrGrad, String unSch, String major) {
      super.Write(ID, Fname, Lname, Grad);
      m_UndergradSchool = unSch;
      m_Major = major;
      YearGraduated = yrGrad;
   }
   public void Display(){
      super.Display();
      System.out.println(" Graduated: " + m_Graduation + " " +
        m_UndergradSchool + " " + m_Major + " " + YearGraduated);
   }
   private YearGraduated;
   private String m_UndergradSchool;
   private String m_Major;
}
```

Each has the member methods `Write()` and `Display()`. The `Write()` method assigns values to instance variables of each class. The `Display()` method displays those values. Though not specifically noted in Chapter 3, each of these classes was actually designed with polymorphism already in mind. Each class contains methods named `Display()` and `Write()` that perform similar tasks, but are done differently. This is polymorphism in action.

Imagine if different names were used for the `Display()` method in each class, such as `StudentDisplay()` and `GradDisplay()`. A programmer who wanted to use these classes would need to memorize the name of each method for each object. This can easily become a challenge, especially if each class has many methods.

Programmers avoid any head scratching over methods and method signatures by performing a little polymorphism magic. They define a method in each class, with the same name, that performs a similar behavior. This requires the programmer to re-member one name that is associated with a behavior. The sample classes (Student and GradStudent) each have their own Display() method.

Figure 4-1 is the Java application class definition of the next program, which shows polymorphism at work. The main() method in Figure 4-1 is practically the same as the main() method of the Java StudentInfo application in Chapter 3. However, there are a few minor modifications.

Definitions of Student class and GradStudent class are contained in the Demo package.

Declare an instance of the Student class.

Declare an instance of the GradStudent class.

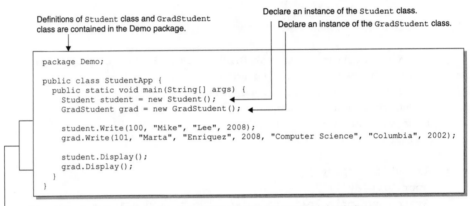

```
package Demo;

public class StudentApp {
   public static void main(String[] args) {
      Student student = new Student();
      GradStudent grad = new GradStudent();

      student.Write(100, "Mike", "Lee", 2008);
      grad.Write(101, "Marta", "Enriquez", 2008, "Computer Science", "Columbia", 2002);

      student.Display();
      grad.Display();
   }
}
```

Polymorphism is used to call the Modify() method and the Display() method of each class.

Figure 4-1   The Display() method in this program is an example of polymorphism.

The first two statements create instances of the Student class and the GradStudent class. The Write() method for each instance is then called to assign values passed as parameters to attributes of the instance.

Polymorphism is used in the last two statements in this example. Both statements call the Display() method. However, because the student object is an instance of the Student class, the Student class's Display() method is called, and be-cause the grad object is an instance of the GradStudent class, the GradStudent class's Display() method is called. Note how the two lines are nearly identical, ex-cept for the instances of their classes.

This is polymorphism at work—one thing (the Display() method) has differ-ent shapes (behaviors, depending on the objects used to call the method). The same can be said about the Write() method because both classes define a Write() method.

Here is the complete Java application that illustrates polymorphism. The application declares an instance of the GradStudent class and then calls the Write() method to write information about a graduate student to instance variables of the Student class and the GradStudent class. The Display() method is then called to display instance variables on the screen.

```java
class StudentInfo {
    public static void main (String args[]) {
        GradStudent myStudent = new GradStudent();
        myStudent.Write(10, 1,"Bob","Smith", 2000,"Columbia University",
            "CS");
        myStudent.Display();
    }
}
class Student
{
    public void Write(int ID, int Grad, String Fname, String Lname) {
        m_ID = ID;
        m_Graduation = Grad;
        m_First = Fname;
        m_Last = Lname;
     }
    public void Display(){
        System.out.println( "Student: " + m_ID + " " + m_First + " " + m_Last
            + " Graduated: " + m_Graduation);
    }
    private int m_ID, m_Graduation;
    private String m_First;
    private String m_Last;
}

class GradStudent extends Student
{
    public void Write(int ID, int Grad, String Fname, String Lname,
int yrGrad, String unSch, String major) {
        super.Write(ID, Fname, Lname, Grad);
        m_UndergradSchool = unSch;
        m_Major = major;
        YearGraduated = yrGrad;
     }
    public void Display(){
      super.Display();
        System.out.println(" Graduated: " + m_Graduation + " " +
            m_UndergradSchool + " " + m_Major + " " + YearGraduated);
```

```
    }
    private YearGraduated;
    private String m_UndergradSchool;
    private String m_Major;
}
```

Overloading Methods

Overloading is another one of those terms you hear used in conjunction with polymorphism. It means that two or more methods are defined using the same name, but with different argument lists. Overloading methods provides us with a way to define similar behavior to work with different types of data by writing a version of a method for each data type that is used.

Any variation in the argument list makes a method distinct from other methods of the same name. That is, the number of arguments, the data type of arguments, and the order in which arguments appear are considered different argument lists.

Let's say that you want to display attributes of the Student class and attributes of the GradStudent class. You could define two methods called Display() that are not associated with either class. One of these methods requires an instance of the Student class as its argument. The other method requires an instance of the GradStudent class as its argument. The second definition of the Display() method is said to *overload* the first definition of the Display() method.

The programmer simply calls the Display() method and passes it either the instance of the Student class or the instance of the GradStudent class. The compiler determines which version of Display() to use by the object passed to the Display() method.

The following example defines two versions of the Display() method. The first version requires an instance of the Student class as its argument list. The second version requires an instance of the GradStudent class. Each version calls the instance's Display() method to display attributes of the instance.

```
public static void Display( Student s ) {
    s.Display();
  }
  public static void Display( GradStudent g ) {
    g.Display();
  }
```

Because these examples might be found in the StudentApp class (not Student or GradStudent), we may opt to make them *static*. By making them static, we indicate that the methods can work on their own and that we don't need to declare a StudentApp object to use them.

Polymorphism Using C++

The previous example uses Java to illustrate polymorphism. Polymorphism can also be implemented using C++, which is shown in the next example. This C++ program defines a `Student` class and a `GradStudent` class. The `GradStudent` class inherits the `Student` class.

Both class definitions define a `Write()` member function and a `Display()` member function, similar to the previous Java program. The `Write()` member function assigns values of its argument list to attributes of the class. The `Display()` member function displays those attributes on the screen.

The `Student` class contains attributes that are common to all students: a student ID, the student name, and an indication of whether the student has graduated. The `GradStudent` class has attributes that pertain to a graduate student. These are the name of the student's undergraduate school, the year the student received an undergraduate degree, and the student's undergraduate major. The `GradStudent` class also can access protected attributes of the `Student` class because the `GradStudent` class inherits the `Student` class.

As with the Java example, the `GradStudent` class's `Display` method calls the `Student` base class's `Display` method to reuse code. Also, the signatures of the `Display` method in `Student` and `GradStudent` are identical.

The `main()` function contains the actual C++ program, which is practically the same program as the `main()` method in the Java example. The first two statements declare an instance of the `Student` class and the `GradStudent` class. The next two statements use those instances to call the `Write()` method of each instance, passing it information about students. The last two statements call the `Display()` function for the respective classes. Also, as with the Java program, the compiler uses the appropriate function for the given class.

Here is the output of the following program:

ID: 100

First: Harry

Last: Kim

Graduation: 2008

ID: 101

First: Elizabeth

Last: Jones

Graduation: 2008

Major: Comp Sci

Undergrad school: Columbia

Undergrad graduation: 2002

```cpp
#include <iostream>
#include <string.h>
using namespace std;
class Student
{
    protected:
        int m_Graduation, m_ID;
        char m_First[16], m_Last[16];
    public:
        void Display()
        {
            cout << "ID: " << m_ID << endl;
            cout << "First: " << m_First << endl;
            cout << "Last: " << m_Last << endl;
            cout << "Graduation: " << m_Graduation << endl;
        }
        void Write( int ID, char First[], char Last[], int Graduation )
        {
            m_ID = ID;
            strcpy( m_First, First );
            strcpy( m_Last, Last );
            m_Graduation = Graduation;
        }
        Student()
        {
            m_ID = m_Graduation = 0;
            m_First[0] = m_Last[0] = '\0';
        }
};

class GradStudent : public Student
{
    protected:
        int m_UndergradGraduation;
        char m_UndergradSchool[64];
        char m_Major[64];
    public:
```

```
        GradStudent()
        {
            m_UndergradGraduation=0;
            m_UndergradSchool[0] = m_Major[0] = '\0';
        }
        void Write( int ID, char First[], char Last[], int Graduation,
            char  Major[], char  UndergradSchool[], int UndergradGraduation )
        {
            Student::Write( ID, First, Last, Graduation );
            strcpy( m_Major, Major );
            strcpy( m_UndergradSchool, UndergradSchool );
            m_UndergradGraduation = UndergradGraduation;
        }
        void Display()
        {
            Student::Display();
            cout << "Major: " << m_Major << endl;
            cout << "Undergrad school: " << m_UndergradSchool << endl;
            cout << "Undergrad graduation: " << m_UndergradGraduation <<
                endl;
        }
};


int main()
{
    Student student;
    GradStudent gradStudent;
    student.Write( 100, "Harry", "Kim", 2008 );
    gradStudent.Write( 101, "Elizabeth", "Jones", 2008, "Comp Sci",
        "Columbia", 2002 );
    student.Display();
    gradStudent.Display();
    return 0;
}
```

An important benefit of polymorphism is that it gives programmers the ability to develop interfaces for complex applications. You've probably heard the term *interface* used in connection with Application Programming Interface (API), which you use to build applications. An API consists of classes and methods used to perform complex behaviors within your program. You simply invoke appropriate classes and methods within your program to perform corresponding behaviors, and you don't have to worry about how those behaviors are actually performed because the API takes care of that for you.

Interface

Think of an *interface* as a go-between, much like your television remote control. When you press the On button, the remote control relays your request to the appropriate component on the television. The component handles all the complexities involved in powering up your television.

You also use the same On button on the same remote control to turn on your VCR, DVD player, and other televisions. The remote control is programmed to know how to relay your request to these other devices. You only need to learn how to use buttons on the remote control. You don't need to learn what happens after you press a remote control button.

The remote control is an interface. Buttons on the remote control are methods, and pressing a button is calling a method. Each button is a form of polymorphism and, in a sense, is overloaded. That is, you press the same On button to turn on the television, VCR, and DVD player. The remote control knows which device to turn on (behavior) by the other buttons you press on the remote control (argument list). For example, if you press the VCR button and then the On button, the remote control knows to turn on the VCR.

Interface Design

Some companies have standard interfaces for objects and behaviors that are shared among applications within their firm. A *standard interface* specifies a method name, argument list, return value, and behavior.

For example, we can say that the Display() method is an interface used to display attributes of objects. Previously in this chapter, you saw two examples of Display() methods: member functions, and static or non-class methods that were overloaded. For the overloaded examples, the name of the method is Display(), and it has one argument—a reference to an object. The behavior of the Display() method is to display attributes of the object passed to it.

An application programmer who wants to display attributes of an object calls the Display() method for the class, or the static/non-member Display method, and passes it a reference to an object. The application programmer is not concerned how the Display() method displays those attributes.

The programmer who designs the object used by the application programmer must define a method that adheres to the interface standard. The object and the method are then provided to the application programmer. The application programmer then uses the interface to call the behavior from within the program.

Some programmers refer to polymorphism as "one interface that has multiple methods." The interface enables an application programmer to enlist a general behavior while the situation determines the exact behavior that is performed. For example, in the static method examples, `Display()` is the general behavior, and the object passed to the `Display()` method is the situation that determines which version of the `Display()` method is called.

The application programmer must know only the general behavior needed to be performed by the program and then call the appropriate interface. The compiler then takes over and determines the specific behavior to perform.

Binding

Every time you call a method in your application, the call to the method must be associated with the method definition. Programmers refer to this as *binding*. Binding occurs either at compile time or at run time. Binding at compile time is called *early binding* and is performed if all the information needed to invoke the method is known when the application is compiled. Binding at runtime is called *late binding* and is performed if some information is missing at compile time that is known only when the application runs.

Early binding is used for normal method calls. No time is lost when the program runs because binding is completed when the executable program is created. This is an advantage over late binding.

Late binding is implemented using a virtual function, which is discussed in the next section. A *virtual function* uses a base reference to point to the type of object used by a method. In many situations, the reference to the object is not known until run time. Therefore, binding cannot occur during compile time and must wait until the program runs to bind the method call to the method.

Although late binding causes an application to run slightly slower, late binding enables a program to respond to events that occur during execution. You don't have to write code for contingencies that might occur during run time, which is an important advantage of late binding.

Run-Time Polymorphism

Previously you learned that polymorphism is used by programmers to define a standard interface that enables application programmers to invoke common behaviors by calling the same method name. You also learned that late binding provides flexibility for a program to respond to events occurring while the program executes.

Run-time polymorphism is a way for a programmer to take advantage of the benefits offered by polymorphism and late binding. *Run-time polymorphism* uses virtual functions to create a standard interface and to call the underlying functions. Those function definitions are bound to function calls during run time.

The term *virtual function* is one of those computer terms that is baffling the first few times you hear it used. Let's pick apart the term and review an example to clear up any confusion you might have.

Virtual means that something appears to be real, but isn't real. For example, a flight simulator lets you fly a virtual airplane. The airplane isn't really there, but you have the feeling you are flying a real airplane.

In the case of a virtual function, the computer is tricked into thinking a function is defined, but the function doesn't have to be defined at that moment. Instead, the *virtual function* can be a placeholder for the real function. The real function is defined when the program is running.

Run-Time Polymorphism in Action

Examining an example is the best way to understand how run-time polymorphism works. The following example is very similar to the previous C++ example. Both programs write and display information about a student. The previous example is a C++ program that uses overloaded methods to implement polymorphism. The following example is a C++ program that uses virtual functions to implement polymorphism.

Three classes are defined in this example: `Student`, `UndergradStudent`, and `GraduateStudent`. The `Student` class is the base class that is inherited by the other classes in the program. A base class is a class that is inherited by another class, which is called a *derived class*.

The `Student` class defines an attribute called `m_ID` that is used to store the student's ID. It also defines a constructor that receives the student ID in the argument list and assigns the student ID to the `m_ID` attributes. The constructor is called whenever an instance of the class is declared. The last two statements in the `Student` class definition define two virtual functions: `Display()` and `Write()`.

The declaration of a virtual function in C++ consists of the keyword `virtual`, the function signature (name and argument list), and a return value. In Java, methods are virtual by default, unless you use the `final` keyword. Virtual functions may be actual functions or merely placeholders for real functions that derived classes must provide.

If you define a virtual function without a body, that means the derived class must provide it (it has no choice, and the program will not compile otherwise). Classes with such functions are called *abstract classes*, because they aren't complete classes and are more a guideline for creating actual classes. (For example, an abstract class might state "you must create the `Display()` method.") In C++, you can create a virtual function without a body by appending =0 after its signature (also known as a *pure* virtual function). You use the `abstract` keyword in Java to create a virtual function without a body.

The `UndergradStudent` class and `GraduateStudent` class are practically the same except the `Display()` function identifies the student as either an undergraduate or graduate student when student information is shown on the screen. Both classes define a `Write()` function and a `Display()` function. The `Write()` function copies student information received in the argument list to attributes of the class. The `Display()` function displays the contents of those attributes and the student ID attribute in the `Student` class.

The `main()` function is where all the action takes place. The first statement declares a pointer that points to an instance of the `Student` class. The next two statements declare an instance of the `UndergradStudent` class and the `GraduateStudent` class. Notice that the student ID is passed to the constructor of each instance. Each constructor calls the constructor of the `Student` class, which assigns the student ID to the `m_ID` attribute.

Run-time polymorphism is implemented in the next three statements, beginning with the assignment of the address of `uStudent` to the pointer `p`. The pointer is then used with the pointer-to-member (->) operator to point to the function `Write()` and then `Display()`. After attributes of the undergraduate student are displayed, the program assigns the address of `gStudent` to the pointer `p` and then proceeds to call the `Write()` and `Display()` functions.

Here is the output of the next program:

Undergraduate Student: 10 Bob Smith 1

Graduate Student: 23 Mary Jones 1

```cpp
#include <iostream>
#include <string>
using namespace std;
class Student {
   protected:
      int m_ID;
   public:
      Student (int i) {
         m_ID = i;
      }
   virtual void display() = 0;
   virtual void write( int, char[], char[]) = 0;
};
```

```cpp
class UndergradStudent : public Student {
    protected:
        int  m_Graduation;
        char m_First[80];
        char m_Last[80];
    public:
        UndergradStudent(int i) : Student (i) { }
        void write( int Grad, char Fname[], char Lname[]) {
            m_Graduation = Grad;
            strcpy(m_First,Fname);
            strcpy(m_Last, Lname);
        }
        void display() {
            cout << "Undergraduate Student: "<< m_ID << " " << m_First
                <<" " << m_Last << " " << m_Graduation<< endl;
        }
};
class GraduateStudent : public Student {
    protected:
        int  m_Graduation;
        char m_First[80];
        char m_Last[80];
    public:
        GraduateStudent(int i) : Student(i) { }
        void write( int Grad, char Fname[], char Lname[]) {
            m_Graduation = Grad;
            strcpy(m_First,Fname);
            strcpy(m_Last, Lname);
        }
        void display() {
            cout << "Graduate Student: "<< m_ID << " " << m_First <<" " <<
                m_Last << " " << m_Graduation<< endl;
        }
};
int main()
{
    Student * p;
    UndergradStudent uStudent(10);
    GraduateStudent gStudent(23);
    p = &uStudent;
    p->write(1,"Bob","Smith") ;
    p->display();
```

```
   p = &gStudent;
   p->write(1,"Mary","Jones") ;
   p->display();
   return 0;
}
```

Quiz

1. What is polymorphism?
2. How is polymorphism implemented?
3. What is late binding?
4. What is early binding?
5. What is the advantage of run-time polymorphism?
6. What is the advantage of compile-time polymorphism?
7. What is an interface?
8. How does polymorphism enable the implementation of an interface?
9. What is a virtual function?
10. What is overloading a method?

CHAPTER

Inheritance

Life would be so much easier if a long-lost relative left you his multimillion-dollar estate. You could be ahead of the game, picking up where your relative left off by benefiting from his hard work. Get real. You probably have a better chance of becoming President of the United States. However, you can pick up where other programmers left off by inheriting their work into your program. It's not the same as inheriting a multimillion-dollar estate, but inheriting part of a program saves you countless hours of programming—and avoids a lot of head banging. Inheritance is a cornerstone of object-oriented programming and is the topic of this chapter.

Inheritance: The Only Way to Program

Inheritance in object-oriented programming is very similar to the way we inherit characteristics from our parents. Characteristics in object-oriented programming terms are attributes and behaviors of a class—that is, the data and methods of a class.

Biological inheritance creates a hierarchical classification that enables you to trace your heritage to generations of relatives who have come before you. The same is true in object-oriented programming. A hierarchical relationship develops as classes inherit from other classes within a program. You can trace this relationship to determine the origins of a class.

Inheritance is a cornerstone of object-oriented programming because it enables objects to inherit attributes and behaviors from other objects, thereby reducing the amount of new code that must be designed, written, and tested each time a new program is developed.

In Chapter 4, you saw how a graduate student object inherits attributes and behaviors of a student object, which are common to all kinds of students. The programmer who created the graduate student object had to focus on defining attributes and behaviors that are common to a graduate student and not those of a student.

Inheritance provides a way to distribute control for development and maintenance of objects. For example, a programmer might be responsible for creating and maintaining the student object. Another programmer might develop and maintain the graduate student object. Whenever a change occurs that affects all students, those changes are made to the student object and are then inherited by the graduate student object. Only the programmer responsible for the student object needs to address those changes because the graduate student object inherits any changes made to the student object.

Inheritance also provides a way to limit access to attributes and behaviors. Previously in Chapter 4, you learned how the public, private, and protected access specifiers are used to determine parts of the program that can access attributes and behaviors.

Members of a class defined using the *public* access specifier are available to other members of the class, other classes, and to all parts of the program.

Those members defined using the *private* access specifier are only accessible by members of the class. They are unavailable to other classes and other parts of the program. The *protected* access specifier identifies attributes and behaviors that are available to members of the class and available to other classes inherited from it.

The purpose of limiting access to attributes and behaviors is to ensure the integrity of the object by controlling how other classes and parts of the program interact with it. A good example of this was shown in Chapter 4. A member method of the student class must be used to access the names of students. The student first name and last name attributes cannot be accessed directly either by another class or from within the program. The member method contains routines to ensure the integrity of student names.

The Class Hierarchy

The hierarchical relationship between classes is sometimes referred to as a *parent-child relationship*. In a parent-child relationship, the child inherits all attributes and behaviors of the parent, and it uses the parent's access specifier to control how those inherited items are available to other classes or functions.

In C++, the parent is referred to as a *base class,* and the child is called a *derived class*. In Java, the parent is the *super class,* and the child is the *subclass*. Regardless of the terms, the relationship and functionality of a parent class and child class are the same.

Defining a parent-child relationship is intuitive in many situations. For example, it is easy to see how a student is the parent of a graduate student because a graduate student has the same attributes and behaviors of a student, and then some. However, sometimes this relationship is illusive because the relationship isn't clear—and maybe it doesn't exist at all.

Programmers use the "is a" test to determine if a relationship exists between classes. The "is a" test determines if the child "is a" parent. For example, a graduate student "is a" student. If an "is a" relationship makes sense, then a parent-child relationship exists and the child can inherit from the parent. If an "is a" relationship doesn't make sense, then a parent-child relationship doesn't exist and the child cannot inherit from the parent, as in the case of an automobile and airplane. An automobile "is a(n)" airplane? This is non-sense, so you shouldn't attempt to create such a relationship.

Types of Inheritance

You have three ways to implement inheritance in a program: simple inheritance, multiple inheritance, and level inheritance. Each enables a class to access attributes and behaviors of another class using slightly different techniques.

Simple

Simple inheritance occurs when there is one parent-child relationship. That is, one child inherits from one parent. Simple inheritance is shown in Figure 5-1. Two classes are represented in this diagram. These are the `Student` class and the `GradStudent` class. The `Student` class is the parent in this relationship and is inherited by the `GradStudent` class, which is the child.

Inheritance occurs from the parent to the child. A parent class cannot access attributes and behavior of a child class. In Figure 5-1, the `Student` class cannot call the

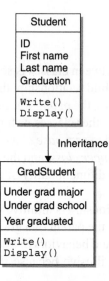

Figure 5-1   Simple inheritance consists of one parent-child relationship. Here, the Student class is the parent and the GradStudent class is the child.

Write() and Display() members of the GradStudent class. However, the GradStudent class can call the Student class's versions of these members.

Multiple

Multiple inheritance occurs when the relationship involves multiple parents and a child. In other words, the child inherits from more than one parent. This is shown in Figure 5-2. In this example, the GradStudent class inherits from both the Person class and the Student class. The Person class and the Student class are both parents to the GradStudent class, which is the child in this relationship.

The GradStudent class inherits the characteristics of a person from the Person class. These are the weight, height, and sex attributes and the Walk() and Sit() methods. You might be wondering how a graduate student walks and sits inside a program. It is difficult to image how this is done. Although we use them in this chapter for illustrative purposes, these behaviors could be programmed into a virtual reality application that shows an animated graduate student walking across campus to a class.

You must keep several factors in mind when implementing multiple inheritance:

- Each class that is inherited must pass the "is a" test. In Figure 5-2, the graduate student must be a student and a person in order to inherit from both parents. If the graduate student fails this test, it cannot inherit from the corresponding parent.

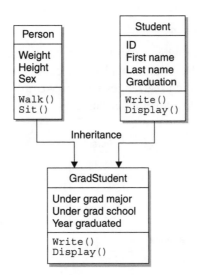

Figure 5-2   Multiple inheritance occurs when one class inherits from two other classes.

- Parent classes are independent of each other. That is, the `Student` class has no knowledge of the `Person` class, and vice versa. The `Student` class cannot access attributes and behaviors of the `Person` class because only the `GradStudent` class inherits from the `Person` class. Likewise, the `Person` class does not inherit from the `Student` class.
- Inheritance occurs in one direction from the parent to the child, which is identical to simple inheritance.
- Any number of parent classes can be inherited by a child class as long as they pass the "is a" test.

NOTE: Multiple inheritance can lead to an interesting and potentially confusing issue referred to as the diamond problem. *Imagine that we have a base class called* IDObject, *which contains an ID attribute to hold a unique ID value. Now, we derive from that class a* Student *and* Instructor *class. So far so good: We have a* Student *and* Instructor *class, both of which have inherited a unique ID attribute. Now, imagine we create a* TeacherAssistant *class multiple derived from* Student *and* Instructor. *This new class has two unique IDs. This is called the* diamond problem *because if we draw the inheritance chart, it will be shaped like a diamond. Though we can make it work, this example can lead to confusion when we want to get the ID for the* TeacherAssistant *class: Which one do we want? Whereas C++ supports multiple inheritance, Java and C# do not. Java and C# provide something called* interfaces, *which are discussed in more detail in the "Multiple Inheritance in Java" section, later in this chapter. As explained in that section, interfaces are different from inheritance.*

Level Inheritance

Level inheritance happens when a child inherits from a parent and then becomes a parent itself to a child. This might sound a little confusing, but it becomes clear by looking at Figure 5-3, which rearranges the Person class, Student class, and GradStudent class into a level inheritance.

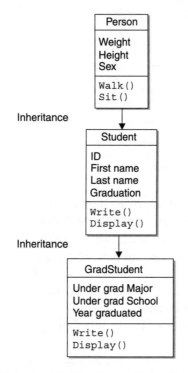

Figure 5-3   Level inheritance occurs when each class inherits one other class as shown here.

The Person class is a parent class that is inherited by the Student class. The Student class is a child class in the Person class–Student class relationship. However, another parent-child relationship exists when the GradStudent class inherits the Student class. In this relationship, the Student class is the parent class, and the GradStudent class is the child class. This means that the Student class has a duel role in inheritance. It is both a child and a parent.

Each parent-child relationship is considered a level. That is, the Person class–Student class relationship is the first level, and the Student class–GradStudent class is the second level. You can have as many levels as required by your program; however, many programmers stop at three levels because it becomes a bit unwieldy to manage beyond three levels.

In level inheritance, the final child class, which is the GradStudent class in the previous example, inherits attributes and behaviors for all classes in the level chain. Here's how this works: The Student class inherits attributes and behaviors from the Person class. Once inherited, these attributes and behaviors are considered members of the Student class, just as if they were defined in the Student class. When the GradStudent class inherits from the Student class, the GradStudent class has access to the Student class's attributes and behavior that now include those inherited from the Person class. As you'll remember, only attributes and behaviors designated as public or protected are inherited.

Although the last child class (that is, the GradStudent class) doesn't directly inherit from the Person class, the Person class still must pass the "is a" test. That is, a graduate student "is a" person.

There is an important difference between multiple inheritance and level inheritance. In multiple inheritance, parent classes are independent of each other. In level inheritance, a parent class that is also a child class (that is, the Student class) can access other parent classes within the leveling chain.

Choosing the Right Type of Inheritance

With three options to choose from, you're probably scratching your head wondering how you will choose. Well, there isn't a magic formula that will provide you with the best choice. Instead, you'll need to use some good-old common sense and apply your knowledge of inheritance to meet your programming objectives.

Deciding when to apply simple inheritance is intuitive because you make this choice when there is only one parent-child relationship between two objects. If you have a child class that inherits a single parent class, then simple inheritance is the only way to go.

Head scratching usually occurs when a child inherits directly or indirectly from more than one parent. This is the case with the GradStudent class, which inherits from both the person class and the student class. Here you have two choices: multiple inheritance and level inheritance.

Some programmers decide which of these to use by determining if there is an "is a" relationship between the two parent classes. For example, is a student a person? If so, then the better choice is to use level inheritance because this maintains the natural relationship between parent classes. That is, other kinds of "student" classes besides GradStudent are likely to inherit the Student class and the Person class. Once the Student class inherits the Person class, all "student" classes inherit the Person class when they inherit the Student class. This is illustrated in Figure 5-4, where the

UndergradStudent, GradStudent, and ContinuingEdStudent classes all inherit the Student class and indirectly inherit the Person class.

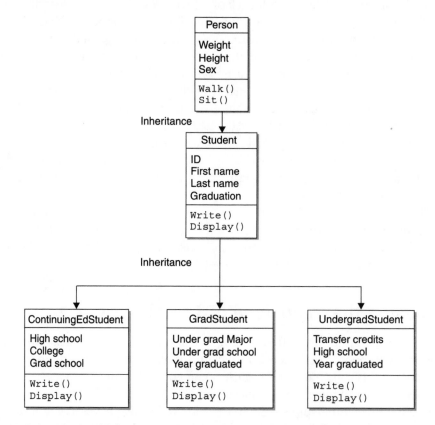

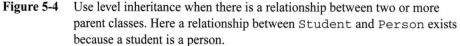

Figure 5-4   Use level inheritance when there is a relationship between two or more parent classes. Here a relationship between Student and Person exists because a student is a person.

In contrast, multiple inheritance is the way to go when there isn't a definitive relationship between two parents. A definitive relationship is when the relationship always passes the "is a" test. If the relationship passes the test sometimes but fails other times, it is not a definitive relationship.

Let's say that an undergraduate student is an athlete and a writer. This means that the UndergradStudent class inherits attributes and behaviors from the Athlete class and the Writer class. However, there isn't a definitive relationship between these two parent classes. That is, an athlete may or may not be a writer, and a writer may or may not be an athlete. This is a clear case where multiple inheritance is the better choice to use in the program, as shown in Figure 5-5.

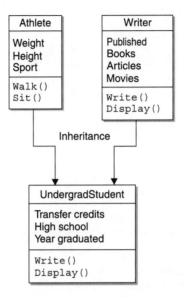

Figure 5-5   Use multiple inherits when there isn't a relationship between two or more parent classes. Here there isn't a relationship between Athlete and Writer.

Simple Inheritance Using C++

Simple inheritance is implemented using C++ by defining two classes. One class is the base class, and the other class is the derived class. Make sure that the derived class passes the "is a" test. That is, the derived class "is a" base class.

The following example illustrates how to use simple inheritance in C++. The two classes defined in this program are the Student class and the GradStudent class. The Student class is the base class, and the GradStudent class is the derived class.

The Student class definition (shown here) contains two member functions: Write() and Display(). Both of these are defined within the public access specifier section of the class, which means that they can be called from the program and from the derived class.

```
class Student
{
    protected:
```

```
        int m_Graduation, m_ID;
        char m_First[16], m_Last[16];
    public:
        virtual void Display()
            {
                cout << "ID: " << m_ID << endl;
                cout << "First: " << m_First << endl;
                cout << "Last: " << m_Last << endl;
                cout << "Graduation: " << m_Graduation << endl;
            }
        void Write( int ID, char First[], char Last[], int Graduation )
        {
            m_ID = ID;
            strcpy( m_First, First );
            strcpy( m_Last, Last );
            m_Graduation = Graduation;
        }
        Student()
        {
            m_ID = m_Graduation = 0;
            m_First[0] = m_Last[0] = '\0';
        }
};
```

The Write() member function receives student information as arguments that are then assigned to attributes of the Student class. The Display() member function displays the values of those attributes on the screen.

The attributes of the Student class are defined in the protected access specifier section of the class definition. These attributes are the student ID, student name, and whether or not the student graduated.

The GradStudent class definition (shown here) follows the Student class definition in this example. As you'll remember from your C++ course, you specify that a derived class inherits a base class by using the colon, the access specifier (optional), and the name of the base class in the class header. In this example, the GradStudent class is shown inheriting the Student class:

```
class GradStudent : public Student
{
    protected:
        int m_UndergradGraduation;
        char m_UndergradSchool[64];
        char m_Major[64];
    public:
        GradStudent()
```

```
    {
        m_UndergradGraduation=0;
        m_UndergradSchool[0] = m_Major[0] = '\0';
    }
    virtual void Write( int ID, char First[], char Last[], int
Graduation,
        char  Major[], char  UndergradSchool[], int UndergradGraduation )
    {
        Student::Write( ID, First, Last, Graduation );
        strcpy( m_Major, Major );
        strcpy( m_UndergradSchool, UndergradSchool );
        m_UndergradGraduation = UndergradGraduation;
    }
    virtual void Display()
    {
        Student::Display();
        cout << "Major: " << m_Major << endl;
        cout << "Undergrad school: " << m_UndergradSchool << endl;
        cout << "Undergrad graduation: " << m_UndergradGraduation << endl;
    }
};
```

The GradStudent class contains the Write() and Display() member functions in its public access specifier section. Notice that the Write() member function receives both student information and graduate student information as argument. The student information is assigned to attributes of the Student class (using the Student class's Write() method), and graduate student information is assigned to attributes of the GradStudent class. Likewise, the Display() member function of the GradStudent class displays the values assigned to attributes of both classes.

The Write() and Display() member functions of the GradStudent class have access to attributes of the Student class because the Student class is inherited by the GradStudent class and because attributes of the Student class are contained within the protected access specifier of that class.

The GradStudent class defines three attributes that specify the year the student received an undergraduate degree, the name of the undergraduate school, and the student's major. All these attributes are defined within the *private* accessor specifier of the class, making them accessible only to member functions of the GradStudent class.

An instance of the GradStudent object called g and a Student object called s are declared within the main() function of the program. The instance name is then used to call the Write() member function of the GradStudent class and is passed student information. This information is then shown on the screen when the `Display()` member function is called.

Here's what is displayed on the screen when the following program executes:

```
ID: 100
First: Harry
Last: Kim
Graduation: 2008
ID: 101
First: Elizabeth
Last: Jones
Graduation: 2008
Major: Comp Sci
Undergrad school: Columbia
Undergrad graduation: 2002
```

```cpp
#include <iostream>
#include <string.h>
using namespace std;
class Student
{
    protected:
        int m_Graduation, m_ID;
        char m_First[16], m_Last[16];
    public:
        virtual void Display()
          {
             cout << "ID: " << m_ID << endl;
             cout << "First: " << m_First << endl;
             cout << "Last: " << m_Last << endl;
             cout << "Graduation: " << m_Graduation << endl;
          }
        void Write( int ID, char First[], char Last[], int Graduation )
        {
           m_ID = ID;
           strcpy( m_First, First );
           strcpy( m_Last, Last );
           m_Graduation = Graduation;
        }
        Student()
        {
           m_ID = m_Graduation = 0;
```

```
            m_First[0] = m_Last[0] = '\0';
        }
};
class GradStudent : public Student
{
    protected:
        int m_UndergradGraduation;
        char m_UndergradSchool[64];
        char m_Major[64];
    public:
        GradStudent()
        {
            m_UndergradGraduation=0;
            m_UndergradSchool[0] = m_Major[0] = '\0';
        }
        virtual void Write( int ID, char First[], char Last[], int Graduation,
            char  Major[], char  UndergradSchool[], int UndergradGraduation )
        {
            Student::Write( ID, First, Last, Graduation );
            strcpy( m_Major, Major );
            strcpy( m_UndergradSchool, UndergradSchool );
            m_UndergradGraduation = UndergradGraduation;
        }
        virtual void Display()
        {
            Student::Display();
            cout << "Major: " << m_Major << endl;
            cout << "Undergrad school: " << m_UndergradSchool << endl;
            cout << "Undergrad graduation: " << m_UndergradGraduation << endl;
        }
};
int main()
{
    Student s;
    GradStudent g;
    s.Write( 100, "Harry", "Kim", 2008 );
    g.Write( 101, "Elizabeth", "Jones", 2008, "Comp Sci", "Columbia", 2002 );
    s.Display();
    g.Display();
    return 0;
}
```

Simple Inheritance Using Java

Simple inheritance is implemented in a Java application using a technique similar to that used in the C++ example. The Java application must define a super class and a subclass, as shown in the following example. The Student class is the super class, which is the same as a base class in C++. The GradStudent class is the subclass, similar to the derived class in the previous example.

The Student class definition is the same as the Student class definition in C++, except that the access specifiers are placed in each statement and method definition. The GradStudent class definition is very similar to the GradStudent class definition in C++, except for two variations.

First, the extends keyword is used in Java to signify inheritance. The extends keyword must be followed by the name of the super class that is being inherited, which is the Student class in this example.

The other variation is found within the Display() method. The first statement within the Display() method definition calls the Student class's Display() method using the keyword super. You use super whenever you want to reference a member of the super class. In this example, the Student class's Display() method causes values of the Student class attributes to be displayed on the screen. The second statement within the GradStudent class's Display() method definition causes attributes of the GradStudent class to be shown on the screen following the student information.

The main method of this example is identical to the main() function of the C++ version of this application, except this example uses Java syntax to declare an instance of the GradStudent class, which you'll remember from your Java course.

Here's what the following program displays on the screen:

ID: 100
First: Mike
Last: Lee
Graduation: 2008
ID: 101
First: Marta
Last: Enriquez
Graduation: 2008
Major: Computer Science
Undergrad Graduation year: 2002
Undergrad School: Columbia

```
class Student {
    protected int nID, nGraduation;
    protected String sFirst, sLast;
    public Student() {
        nID = 0;
        nGraduation = 0;
        sFirst = new String();
        sLast = new String();
    }
    public void Display() {
        System.out.println("ID: " + nID);
        System.out.println("First: " + sFirst);
        System.out.println("Last: " + sLast);
        System.out.println("Graduation: " + nGraduation);
    }
    public void Write( int ID, String First, String Last, int Graduation ) {
        nID = ID;
        sFirst = First;
        sLast = Last;
        nGraduation = Graduation;
    }
}
class GradStudent extends Student {
    String sMajor, sUndergradSchool;
    int nUndergradGraduation;
    public GradStudent() {
        sMajor = "";
        sUndergradSchool="";
        nUndergradGraduation=0;
    }
    public void Display() {
        super.Display();
        System.out.println("Major: " + sMajor );
        System.out.println("Undergrad Graduation year: " +
            nUndergradGraduation);
        System.out.println("Undergrad School: " + sUndergradSchool );
    }
    public void Write( int ID, String First, String Last, int Graduation,
        String Major, String UndergradSchool, int UndergradGraduation ) {
        super.Write( ID, First, Last, Graduation);
        sUndergradSchool = UndergradSchool;
        sMajor = Major;
        nUndergradGraduation = UndergradGraduation;
```

```
        }
    }
    public class StudentApp {
        public static void main(String[] args) {
            Student s = new Student();
            GradStudent g = new GradStudent();
            s.Write( 100, "Mike", "Lee", 2008);
            g.Write(101, "Marta", "Enriquez", 2008, "Computer Science",
    "Columbia", 2002);
            s.Display();
            g.Display();
        }
        public static void Display( Student s ) {
            s.Display();
        }
        public static void Display( GradStudent g ) {
            g.Display();
        }
    }
```

Level Inheritance Using C++

Level inheritance is implemented in C++ by defining at least three classes. The first two classes have a parent-child relationship, and the second and third classes must also have a parent-child relationship. Each child class must pass the "is a" test in order to inherit from the parent class.

The following example shows level inheritance in a C++ program. Three classes are defined in this example: the Person class, the Student class, and the GradStudent class. The Person class is a base class and is the parent in the parent-child relationship with the Student class. The Student class is the derived class in this relationship. That is, the Student class inherits from the Person class.

The Person class defines two member functions within the public access specific section of the class definition. These are Write() and Display(). The Write() member function assigns information about a person that is received as arguments to the attributes of the class. The Display() member function shows values of those attributes on the screen.

Both the Student class definition and the GradStudent class definition are the same, as you saw in the "Simple Inheritance Using C++" section of this chapter.

However, you'll notice that the Student class inherits from the Person class and that the GradStudent class inherits from the Student class.

The Student class is both a derived class and a base class. It is a derived class in the parent-child relationship with the Person class, and it is a base class in the parent-child relationship with the GradStudent class.

Look carefully at the definitions of the Write() member function and Display() member function of the GradStudent class and you'll notice that both member functions access methods of the Person class and the Student class. This is made possible by level inheritance.

The Student class inherits members of the Person class that are defined in the public and protected access specifier sections of the Person class. This inheritance is passed along to the GradStudent class when the GradStudent class inherits from the Student class. Any member of the Person class that is accessible to the Student class is also accessible to the GradStudent class.

The main() function of this example is nearly identical to the main() function of the simple inheritance example, except the Write() member function is passed information about the person as well as about the student and the graduate student.

Here is the output of the following program:

```
ID: 100
First: Harry
Last: Kim
Graduation: 2008
ID: 101
First: Elizabeth
Last: Jones
Graduation: 2008
Major: Comp Sci
Undergrad school: Columbia
Undergrad graduation: 2002
```

```
#include <iostream>
#include <string.h>
using namespace std;
class Person
{
    protected:
        int m_ID;
        char m_First[16], m_Last[16];
    public:
        Person()
        {
```

```
            m_ID = 0;
            m_First[0] = m_Last[0] = '\0';
        }
        virtual void Display()
        {
            cout << "ID: " << m_ID << endl;
            cout << "First: " << m_First << endl;
            cout << "Last: " << m_Last << endl;
        }
        void Write( int ID, char First[], char Last[] )
        {
            m_ID = ID;
            strcpy( m_First, First );
            strcpy( m_Last, Last );
        }
};
class Student : public Person
{
    protected:
        int m_Graduation;
    public:
        virtual void Display()
        {
            Person::Display();
            cout << "Graduation: " << m_Graduation << endl;
        }
        void Write( int ID, char First[], char Last[], int Graduation )
        {
            Person::Write( ID, First, Last );
            m_Graduation = Graduation;
        }
        Student()
        {
            m_Graduation = 0;
        }
};
class GradStudent : public Student
{
    protected:
        int m_UndergradGraduation;
        char m_UndergradSchool[64];
        char m_Major[64];
    public:
        GradStudent()
```

```
    {
        m_UndergradGraduation=0;
        m_UndergradSchool[0] = m_Major[0] = '\0';
    }
    virtual void Write( int ID, char First[], char Last[], int Graduation,
        char  Major[], char  UndergradSchool[], int UndergradGraduation )
    {
        Student::Write( ID, First, Last, Graduation );
        strcpy( m_Major, Major );
        strcpy( m_UndergradSchool, UndergradSchool );
        m_UndergradGraduation = UndergradGraduation;
    }
    virtual void Display()
    {
        Student::Display();
        cout << "Major: " << m_Major << endl;
        cout << "Undergrad school: " << m_UndergradSchool << endl;
        cout << "Undergrad graduation: " << m_UndergradGraduation << endl;
    }
};
int main()
{
    Student s;
    GradStudent g;
    s.Write( 100, "Harry", "Kim", 2008 );
    g.Write( 101, "Elizabeth", "Jones", 2008, "Comp Sci", "Columbia", 2002 );
    s.Display();
    g.Display();
    return 0;
}
```

Level Inheritance Using Java

Java implements level inheritance very similarly to how level inheritance is implemented in C++, as shown in this next example. The same three classes defined in the C++ program are also defined in this Java application. Each class has the same attributes and member methods that perform the same functionality as their counterparts in the C++ program.

The Person class is inherited by the Student class using the keyword extends. The Student class is inherited by the GradStudent class also using the keyword extends. The Display() method of the Student class and of the

`GradStudent` class each call the `Display()` method of its super class in order to display values of the super class's attributes. This is similar to how attributes of a super class are displayed in simple inheritance using Java.

The `main()` method in this example contains practically the same statements found in the simple inheritance example, except the `Write()` method is passed information about a person as well as information about a student and a graduate student. The `Display()` method within the `main()` method displays values of attributes of all the classes on the screen.

Here is what is displayed on the screen when you run the following program:

ID: 100
First: Mike
Last: Lee
Graduation: 2008
ID: 101
First: Marta
Last: Enriquez
Graduation: 2008
Major: Computer Science
Undergrad Graduation year: 2002
Undergrad School: Columbia

```
class Person {
   protected int nID;
   protected String sFirst, sLast;
   public Person() {
      nID = 0;
      sFirst = "";
      sLast = "";
   }
   public void Display() {
      System.out.println("ID: " + nID);
      System.out.println("First: " + sFirst);
      System.out.println("Last: " + sLast);
   }
   public void Write( int ID, String First, String Last ) {
      nID = ID;
      sFirst = First;
      sLast = Last;
   }
}
class Student extends Person{
   protected int nGraduation;
```

```
    public Student() {
      nGraduation = 0;
    }
    public void Display() {
        super.Display();
        System.out.println("Graduation: " + nGraduation);
    }
    public void Write( int ID, String First, String Last, int Graduation ) {
        super.Write(ID, First, Last);
        nGraduation = Graduation;
    }
}
class GradStudent extends Student {
    String sMajor, sUndergradSchool;
    int nUndergradGraduation;
    public GradStudent() {
        sMajor = "";
        sUndergradSchool="";
        nUndergradGraduation=0;
    }
    public void Display() {
        super.Display();
        System.out.println("Major: " + sMajor );
        System.out.println("Undergrad Graduation year: " +
          nUndergradGraduation);
        System.out.println("Undergrad School: " + sUndergradSchool );
    }
    public void Write( int ID, String First, String Last, int Graduation,
        String Major, String UndergradSchool, int UndergradGraduation ) {
        super.Write( ID, First, Last, Graduation);
        sUndergradSchool = UndergradSchool;
        sMajor = Major;
        nUndergradGraduation = UndergradGraduation;
    }
}
public class StudentApp {
    public static void main(String[] args) {
        Student s = new Student();
        GradStudent g = new GradStudent();
        s.Write( 100, "Mike", "Lee", 2008);
        g.Write(101, "Marta", "Enriquez", 2008, "Computer Science",
"Columbia", 2002);
        s.Display();
        g.Display();
```

```
    }
    public static void Display( Student s ) {
        s.Display();
    }
    public static void Display( GradStudent g ) {
        g.Display();
    }
}
```

Multiple Inheritance Using C++

Previously in this chapter you learned that multiple inheritance is a way for a child to inherit from two unrelated parents. The example in this section shows how to implement multiple inheritance using C++.

This example introduces two new classes: `Instructor` and `Worker`. The `Worker` class contains attributes and methods for working with an income attribute. The `Instructor` class is derived from the `Person` class (inheriting the ID and the first and last name attributes and methods) as well as the `Worker` class. This is done to emphasize that a worker need not be a person to generate an income (for example, the worker could be a vending machine). However, an instructor is both a person and an income producer, so we use multiple inheritance.

The `Instructor` class has a parent-child relationship with both the `Person` class and the `Worker` class. The `Person` class and the `Worker` class are both base classes, and the `Instructor` class is the derived class.

Multiple inheritance is specified in the class header of the derived class, as shown in the `Instructor` class definition of this example. The class names of classes inherited by the derived class are specified to the right of the colon after the accessor specifier. Each class inherited by the Instructor class must be separated by a comma.

The result of this program is the same as the level inheritance example. The `Write()` member function of the `Instructor` class is passed information for all classes. The `Display()` member function is called to display those values on the screen.

Here is what is displayed on the screen when you run the following program:

ID: 102
First: Marcos
Last: Lopez
Income: 100000
Tenured: Yes

```cpp
#include <iostream>
#include <string.h>
using namespace std;
class Person
{
    protected:
        int m_ID;
        char m_First[16], m_Last[16];
    public:
        Person()
        {
            m_ID = 0;
            m_First[0] = m_Last[0] = '\0';
        }
        virtual void Display()
        {
            cout << "ID: " << m_ID << endl;
            cout << "First: " << m_First << endl;
            cout << "Last: " << m_Last << endl;
        }
        void Write( int ID, char First[], char Last[] )
        {
            m_ID = ID;
            strcpy( m_First, First );
            strcpy( m_Last, Last );
        }
};
class Worker
{
    protected:
        int m_Income;
    public:
        Worker()
        {
            m_Income = 0;
        }
        void Write( int Income )
        {
            m_Income = Income;
        }
        void Display()
        {
            cout << "Income: " << m_Income << endl;
        }
```

```
};
class Instructor : public Person, public Worker
{
    protected:
        bool m_Tenured;
    public:
        Instructor()
        {
            m_Tenured = false;
        }
        void Write( int ID, char First[], char Last[], bool Tenured,
         int Salary )
        {
            Person::Write( ID, First, Last );
            Worker::Write( Salary );
            m_Tenured = Tenured;
        }
        void Display()
        {
            Person::Display();
            Worker::Display();
            cout << "Tenured: " << (m_Tenured?"Yes":"No") << endl;
        }
};
int main()
{
    Instructor i;
    i.Write( 102, "Marcos", "Lopez", true, 100000 );
    i.Display();
    return 0;
}
```

Multiple Inheritance Using Java

Multiple inheritance is not supported in Java. Therefore, you'll need to use level inheritance whenever you want a class to inherit from two or more other classes. Remember that each class must pass the "is a" test. Any class that fails this test should not be used in level inheritance.

Java instead provides *interfaces,* which can in some ways act or seem like multiple inheritance. However, an interface is best thought of as something like a purely abstract class. That is to say, it declares the names of member functions but doesn't actually provide any reusable code from which you can employ inheritance. If you implement an interface in a Java class, you must create all the needed code yourself for those functions. For this reason, interfaces are not really a part of inheritance.

Interfaces should really be considered a set of promises. If a class implements an interface (and therefore contains all the code needed to implement it), then other objects can communicate or work with the class via the interface.

Quiz

1. What is inheritance?
2. What is simple inheritance?
3. What is level inheritance?
4. What is multiple inheritance?
5. What is the "is a" test?
6. When would you use multiple inheritance?
7. When would you use level inheritance?
8. What is the maximum number of levels in level inheritance?
9. What members of a class can another class inherit?
10. What is the difference between base class/derived class and super class/subclass?

Abstraction

You probably heard the story of the multimillionaire who told her son that he would inherit the family fortune if he promised to continue working after she passed on. Mom dies. The money starts pouring in, and somehow the son forgets about his promise. However, a clause in her will forces him back to work. So what does this have to do with abstraction? It *is* abstraction! Abstraction is a way a programmer of a super class (mom) forces a programmer of a subclass (son) to define a behavior. You'll learn about the whys and hows of abstraction in this chapter.

Abstraction: The Enforcer

Let's begin exploring abstraction by revisiting the concepts *class*, *super class*, and *subclass*, which you learned about in Chapter 5. A class contains data and behaviors that are associated with an object. For example, a student ID is data, and register-ing a student is a behavior that is likely to be found in a Student class.

Programmers define a super class whenever two or more objects use data and a behavior. A super class is Java's version of a base class in C++. The super class is then inherited by other classes that require the data and behavior. These classes are called *subclasses* in Java and *derived* classes in C++.

For example, the UndergradStudent class and the GradStudent class are likely to inherit the Student class in order to access the student ID and registration behavior, as well as other data and behaviors defined in the Student class (see Figure 6-1).

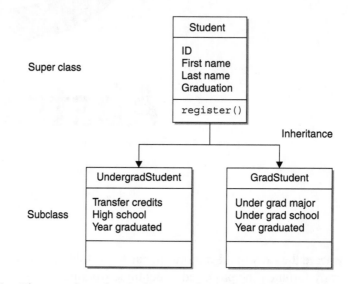

Figure 6-1   The Student class is the super class and is inherited by the UndergradStudent class and the GradStudent class, which are subclasses.

To avoid confusion, we'll use the terms *super class* and *subclass* in this chapter, but everything we say about them also applies to a base class and derived class in C++.

A behavior defined in a super class is referred to as *default* behavior because it specifies instructions that are followed by all subclasses that use the behavior. A programmer who defines a subclass has the option of using a default behavior or redefining the behavior to suit the needs of the subclass.

Let's say that graduate students have an entirely different registration process than other students. Therefore, the default registration behavior in the super class cannot be used by the subclass. The programmer who defines the subclass ignores the default registration behavior and defines a new registration behavior that is specifically designed for a graduate student. (You learned how this is done in Chapter 5.)

This seems a sound decision, but suppose the programmer of a subclass forgets to redefine the registration behavior and uses the default behavior instead. The default registration behavior performs, but it registers the graduate student using the default registration process. The graduate student is registered, although improperly, because the programmer forgot to define the registration behavior for a graduate student. The default registration process may not address any idiosyncrasies required to register a graduate student.

Function vs. Functionality

Sometimes a behavior is common to multiple subclasses, but there isn't a default set of instructions to use to perform the behavior. For example, the registration process might be different for each category of student. This means the `UndergradStudent` class has a different registration process than the `GradStudent` class, but both classes must have a registration behavior (see Figure 6-2).

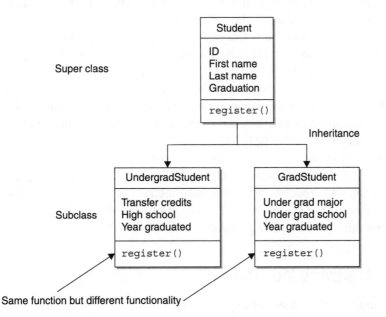

Figure 6-2   Both subclasses have the same function but each has different functionality.

Programmers distinguish a behavior from instructions used to perform the behavior using the terms *function* and *functionality*. A function is a behavior. This is like

the registration process. Functionality is the set of instructions used to perform the behavior. These are the steps used to register a student. Programmers make this distinction in order to implement abstraction.

The Power of Abstraction

Abstraction is the technique used by the programmer of a super class to require that programmers of its subclasses define the functionality of a behavior. Let's return to the example of the `Student` class and the `GradStudent` class to see how this works.

The programmer of the `GradStudent` class must redefine the registration function that is defined in the `Student` class because the registration function defined by the `Student` class is inappropriate for a graduate student.

There is the possibility that the programmer will forget to define a new registration function and use the default registration function instead. However, the programmer can be forced to define the registration function if the programmer of the super class makes the super class an abstract class.

An *abstract* class is a class that cannot be instantiated. That is, you cannot declare an instance of an abstract class. An abstract class must be inherited by a subclass in order for its data and behavior to be used in an application.

An abstract class can contain member methods (Java) or member functions (C++) that are designated by the programmer of the super class as abstract. This requires that the programmer of a subclass redefine the abstract method (function); otherwise, a compile error is displayed.

For example, the `Student` class can be designed as an abstract class and its registration method can be an abstract method. The programmer of the `GradStudent` class is forced to redefine the registration method in order to successfully compile the application (see Figure 6-3). You might say that abstraction is a way to remind a programmer of the missing method.

The Abstract Method

An abstract method does not require instructions because instructions are provided in the redefined method contained in the subclass. However, the programmer of the super class must define an empty abstract method as a member of the abstract class.

Some programmers look at this as specifying a required behavior (function) without defining how the behavior is performed (functionality). The subclass defines how the behavior is performed.

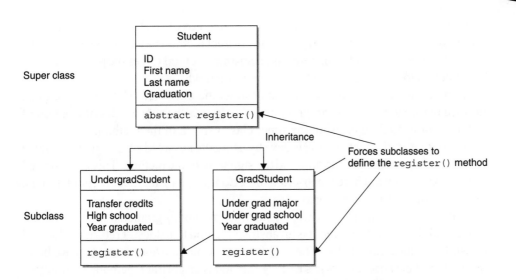

Figure 6-3   Subclasses must define all abstract methods of the super class.

For example, the programmer of the Student class tells programmers of subclasses that they must define a registration process by defining an abstract registration method in the super class. It is the job of the programmer of the GradStudent class to define instructions on how to register a graduate student.

In other words, the programmer of the super class specifies that there must be a registration function, and the programmer of the subclass defines its functionality.

Abstraction in Action

An abstraction is implemented by defining an abstract class using the abstract keyword in Java. This is shown in the following example, which defines the Student class as an abstract class. Remember that you cannot create an instance of any class designated as an abstract class. This means that you cannot declare an instance of the Student class. The Student class must be inherited by a subclass, which is shown later in this section.

```
abstract class Student
{

}
```

You can define data members and member methods of an abstract class. Member methods may or may not be designated an abstract method based on the needs of the class. A member method designated as an abstract method forces the programmer of the subclass to redefine the abstract member method.

Member methods not designated an abstract member method do not have to be defined in the subclass. The programmer who defines the subclass has the option of redefining the method or using the super class version of the method.

You define an abstract method in Java by using the keyword abstract followed by the data type of the return value and the signature of the method. This is illustrated in the next example, where we inserted the register() member method into the definition of the Student class.

In this example, the register() member method is granted public access using the public access specifier. It is an abstract method that doesn't return a value and doesn't have an argument list. The register() method also doesn't have a body defined for it because the register() method is an abstract method. The body of an abstract method is defined when the method is redefined by a subclass.

After the following Java example is the equivalent in C++, using a *pure virtual* function. A pure virtual function in C++ is indicated with the special =0 postfix, which identifies it as an abstract method, and the class it is in becomes an abstract class.

```
//Java
abstract class Student
{
    public abstract void register();
}

//C++
class Student   // C++ example
{
public:
    virtual void register() =0 ;
}
```

The subclass definition must inherit the super class and define any methods that are designated abstract in the super class. This is shown in the following example, where the GradStudent class inherits the Student class by using the extends keyword.

Notice that the register() method is defined within the GradStudent class. The programmer who defined the GradStudent class doesn't have any alternative but to define the register() method. Failure to do so causes a compile error, which you'll see in the next section.

We purposely kept the `register()` method simple by having it display a one-line message on the screen when the method is invoked. You can easily use this example as a model for more complex methods in your own applications:

```
class GradStudent extends Student{
    public void register() {
        System.out.print("Graduate Student Registered.");
    }
```

The application can only declare an instance of the subclass, which is the `GradStudent` class in this example. Furthermore, only the `register()` method defined in the `GradStudent` class can be called from within the application, as shown in the next example. You cannot call the `register()` method defined in the `Student` class because that method is an abstract method and cannot be directly accessed from the application.

```
class AbstractDemo {
    public static void main (String args[]) {
        GradStudent myGradStudent = new GradStudent();
        myGradStudent.register();
    }
}
```

Here is the complete Java application that uses an abstract class and abstract member method. The first statement within the `main()` method uses the new operator to declare an instance of the `GradStudent`class. It also declares a reference to the `GradStudent` class, which is assigned the location of the instance.

The next statement calls the `register()` method of the `GradStudent` class, which displays a message on the screen saying that the graduate student has been registered.

```
class AbstractDemo {
    public static void main (String args[]) {
        GradStudent myGradStudent = new GradStudent();
        myGradStudent.register();
    }
}
abstract class Student
{
    public abstract void register();
}
class GradStudent extends Student{
    public void register() {
        System.out.print("Graduate Student Registered.");
```

```
    }
}
```

A similar example in C++ of a derived class that provides the required "pure vir-tual" (abstract) method, as dictated by its base class, would look like the following:

```
class GradStudent : public Student{
    public:
        void register() {
            cout << "Graduate Student Registered."<<endl;
        }
    }
}
```

Errors Galore

Expect compiler errors whenever abstraction is used in an application, but look upon those errors as a good thing. The purpose of abstraction is to force a programmer to de-fine a method that is designated as an abstract method in a super class. Abstraction is also used to prevent an instance of a super class from being declared in an application.

The reason for imposing these limitations is because the abstract class has some but not necessarily all the detail needed to implement default methods. In previous examples, you saw that the Student class requires a registration procedure but doesn't have sufficient information to define details of that procedure. Programmers of subclasses that inherit the Student class provide those details.

Three common errors occur when abstraction is used:

- The failure of the programmer to define an abstract method in a subclass
- An attempt by the programmer to call the super class's abstract method
- An attempt to declare an instance of the abstract super class in the program

Let's take a look at how failure to define an abstract method in a subclass can cause a compiler error. The next example is similar to other applications used in this chapter. It defines the Student class as an abstract class that contains the register() method, which is designated as an abstract method.

The programmer of the GradStudent class is expected to define details of the register() method, but the programmer decides not to do so because the register() method isn't called in the program (see Figure 6-4). You'll notice this in the main() method, where the program simply creates an instance of the GradStudent class.

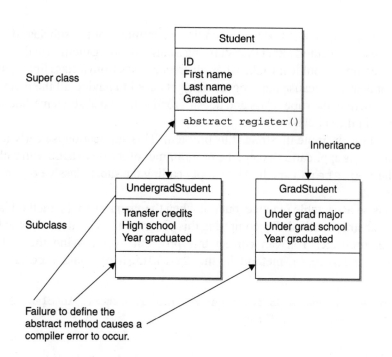

Figure 6-4   Failure to define the abstract member in a subclass causes a compiler error.

Try compiling this program and you'll discover that the compiler complains because the `register()` method is defined in the `GradStudent` class. You'll probably see an error message similar to this:

```
class GradStudent must be declared abstract. It does not
define void register() from class Student.
```

You can fix this problem by defining a `register()` method in the `GradStudent` class definition and then recompiling the program, like so:

```
class AbstractDemo {
   public static void main (String args[]) {
      GradStudent myGradStudent = new GradStudent();
   }
}
abstract class Student
{
   public abstract void register();
}
class GradStudent extends Student{
}
```

Another common error occurs when the programmer of the subclass decides to call the abstract method rather than defining a corresponding method in the subclass. This is a common rookie mistake when abstract classes from a class library are used in an application because the programmer gets used to having all the methods defined for them in the super class and doesn't realize that an abstract method must be redefined in the subclass.

The follow example illustrates this problem. This application is nearly identical to the previous application except the programmer of the GradStudent class defines the register() method by simply calling the super class's register() method.

This is an acceptable practice, but not when the register() method is designated an abstract method. Try compiling this program and you'll receive the following error message. You can correct this problem by removing the call to the super.register() method in the GradStudent class's register() method.

```
Can't directly invoke abstract method void register() in class Student.
        super.register();
                 ^
```

```
class AbstractDemo {
    public static void main (String args[]) {
        GradStudent myGradStudent = new GradStudent();
        myGradStudent.register();
    }
}
abstract class Student
{
    public abstract void register();
}
class GradStudent extends Student{
    public void register() {
        super.register();
    }
}
```

The third common error that some programmers experience when using abstraction is to attempt to declare an instance of an abstract class. This is shown in the next example, where the programmer declares an instance of the Student class, called myStudent, in the second statement of the main() method.

You've seen a similar statement used successfully in Chapter 4. This statement would also be successful here if it weren't for the fact that the Student class is an abstract class. You simply cannot declare an instance of an abstract class.

Try compiling this program, and you receive the following error message:

```
class Student is an abstract class. It can't be instantiated.
        Student myStudent = new Student();
```

You can correct this error by removing the second statement in the `main()` method, thereby not attempting to declare an instance of the `Student` class, as shown here:

```
class AbstractDemo {
   public static void main (String args[]) {
      GradStudent myGradStudent = new GradStudent();
      Student myStudent = new Student();
      myGradStudent.register();
   }
}
abstract class Student
{
   public abstract void register();
}

class GradStudent extends Student{
  public void register() {
     System.out.print("Graduate Student Registered.");
  }
}
```

Frameworks, Libraries, and Abstraction

Abstraction is sometimes a game of guessing the future. You try to design a class, or set of classes, that will hopefully be in use for several years. How can you predict today what can be useful tomorrow? The answer is, of course, experience. As you develop more experience in working with classes, you start to see how the OO paradigm works. Also, you start to appreciate the tools it provides.

There are times when a decision is made that might seem to defeat the purpose of a single class. These are usually the times when a single class isn't really the goal, but really an entire class library or framework is the important part. Put another way, you may find yourself writing a class that requires you to implement certain abstract methods from a base class that simply might not make sense.

If you look at it on the basis of just your class, it might seem silly. But, if you consider the larger picture of the framework or library, it will start to make sense. Let's

take a look at a perfectly good example in Java: the `String` class and its `toString` method.

Java has a `String` class, which contains, of course, a string. Now, in this `String` class is a method called `toString`. And what does `toString` give us? A string that represents our data. How silly is that? A String class that has a method to return a string variable.

Turns out, it's really not silly at all, but quit ingenious if we look at the Java Library. See, `toString` isn't just part of the `String` class, it's part of the `Object` class from which all Java classes are derived. This means that `toString` is really defined for all Java objects. This is exceptionally cool when we consider that for debugging purposes we should be able to display the contents of "any" Java object using the following code:

```
System.out.print( AnyObject.toString() ); !
```

We are bypassing a few of the details of implementation, and not showing any actual code, in order to make a point: The needs of the many outweigh the needs of the one. Or, it is often better to design a set of classes with an overall usefulness that a small number of classes might not seem to benefit from. The truth is, we would probably figure out by looking closer at them that they probably all *do* benefit.

Quiz

1. What is abstraction?
2. When should abstraction be used in a program?
3. What is an abstract method?
4. Can an abstract method be called within a program?
5. What happens if an abstract method is not redefined?
6. Can an instance of an abstract class be declared in a program?
7. Can an abstract method be called directly by a subclass?
8. Must an abstract method be redefined by a subclass?
9. Must all methods in an abstract class be designated as abstract?
10. Must all methods in an abstract class be redefined in a subclass?

Identifying and Describing Objects

Object-oriented programming is as easy a playing a game of Password. Fans of the Game Show Network remember the popular game where a player identifies something to another player by describing it. Try playing Password the next time your party hits a lull and you'll see how easy it is—or isn't—to describe something. What does the game Password have to do with object-oriented programming? Both require you to identify an object by describing it. A Password player describes an object to a fellow player, whereas a programmer describes an object to a program in the form of a class definition. Describing an object is a deceivingly simply concept to understand, but one that is difficult to do. We'll show you how the pros do it in this chapter.

An Object

The world would be a difficult place in which to live if we only described things based on their attributes and behaviors like we do when playing the game Password. Think for a moment. How would you describe yourself as a student without using the word *student*? It wouldn't be easy because we don't look at the world as descriptions of things. Instead, everything in our world is viewed as an object.

If someone asks, What do you do? You probably reply by saying you are a student. No further explanation is needed because everyone knows the characteristics of a student. They know you are low on funds, pay tuition, attend classes, do homework, and go to all-night parties to break the tension.

If someone asks, How do you go to school? You probably say that you drive a car. Again, no further explanation is required. Everyone knows what a car is. You don't need to go into a lengthy descriptions of the car you drive.

As you learned at the beginning of this book, object-oriented programming is centered on identifying and describing real-world objects so they can be used by a program the same way that we use objects in real life. Throughout this book you learned how to create objects in C++ and Java programs by defining classes and then declaring instances of those classes in your programs.

We'll switch gears a bit in this chapter and explore techniques object-oriented programmers use to identify and describe real-world objects so that those objects can be encoded into an object-oriented program. Once you've mastered these techniques, you'll be able to translate an object you see around you into one or more classes in your program.

Let's begin our exploration with the definition of an object. An *object* is a person, place, or thing—such as a student, a campus, or a book—that is defined by an object name, attributes, and behaviors.

An *object name* is the name of an object, such as student, campus, or book. An *attribute* is information about the object, such as a student name (Bob Smith), the name of a campus (Morningside Heights campus), or the title of a book (Object-Oriented Programming Demystified). A *behavior* is an activity that is associated with an object. For example, a student registers for class. The campus is open or closed. And the book can be opened or closed.

Identifying Attributes

Some attributes are easy to identify because we use them to describe an object. For example, attributes of a student object are the student's name, home address, home telephone number, and personal e-mail address. You probably can think of other attributes that describe a student.

Other attributes are not obvious. Let's say you are identifying attributes of a window. You are likely to mention the height, length, and width of the window and maybe the color of the window frame. However, you also need to identify the opaqueness of glass and other finer attributes that the average person overlooks when seeing a window. Admittedly you can find yourself going crazy trying to identify all attributes of an object because there are so many of them in a typical object.

Object-oriented programmers determine the number and type of attributes that they need to identify based on the goals of the system they are developing. For example, a college admission system contains a student object. This system needs a set of attributes that identifies a student, provides student contact information, the student's academic record, and recommendations. The system doesn't need the student's complete medical history, psychological profile, or genealogical background.

In contrast, a system that simulates a window, such as a Computer Aided Design application, needs to have sufficient attributes of a window in order to project how the window reacts to different circumstances. For example, the tensile strength of the window is needed in order to depict how the window reacts to hurricanes. Tensile strength is an attribute that is an indicator of how much pressure the window can withstand before breaking.

Therefore, you should determine the needs of your system before embarking on identifying attributes of objects that will be used by your system. Limit your selection of attributes to only those attributes your system requires. This ensures that you spend your time efficiently and identify only the attributes of an object needed by your system.

Describing Attributes

Identifying the proper set of attributes for your system is half the job. You still need to describe each attribute. Think of identifying an attribute as *naming* the attribute, and think of describing an attribute as *assigning* the attribute name a value.

Some descriptions are intuitive, such as using inches to describe the height of a window. Other descriptions are more challenging. For example, how would you describe the color of a window? You might say, the window is white, blue, black, or the name of any color. However, those colors are vague because each of those colors has a hundred or more shades. When you say that the window is blue, you really mean that the window is one of many shades of blue.

Attributes that have subjective values are difficult to describe because the system that you develop requires precise values and not subjective values. Fortunately, there are standard ways of precisely defining subjective values of many attributes. It is your job to learn those standards before you begin identifying attributes. Typically, the business unit who is sponsoring your system can provide you with those standards.

For example, several standards are used to precisely define a color as a unique number. You would use the standard that is appropriate for your system to describe the color attribute of an object.

Decomposing Attributes to Data

Some programmers who are not familiar with object-oriented programming confuse attributes of an object with data associated with an object. Previously you learned that an attribute is information that describes an object. Data is the smallest amount of meaningful information.

This sounds confusing at first, but an example will quickly make this clear. At attribute of a student object is the student's name. However, the student's name isn't the smallest amount of meaningful information. The smallest amount of information is the student's first name, middle name, and last name, each of which is called *data*.

Object-oriented programmers decompose each attribute into data and then use data in the corresponding class definition to describe the object. Decomposition is the technique that reduces an attribute into its data components.

The best way to decompose attributes is to make a two-column list, as show in Table 7-1. List the attribute in the first column and then ask yourself whether the attribute is the smallest amount of meaningful information that describes the object.

If so, then use the attribute as data. For example, the attribute Graduated, shown at the bottom of Table 7-1, is the smallest amount of meaningful information. It cannot be decomposed. Therefore, the attribute is data and is listed in the data column.

Attribute	Data
Student Name	First Name
	Middle Name
	Last Name
Student Address	Street Address 1
	Street Address 2
	City
	State
	Zip Code
Graduated	Graduated

Table 7-1   Decomposing Attributes to Data

If the attribute is not the smallest amount of meaningful information, then decompose (break down) the attribute into its data components. Table 7-1 illustrates the decomposition of the Student Name and Student Address attributes.

Identifying Behaviors

A behavior of an object is something an object does. Some behaviors are obvious and easy to identify, such as a student registering for a course. Other behaviors are less obvious and can be illusive to identify, such as how a window behaves when the full force of a hurricane bears down on the window glass.

You can imagine that an object performs hundreds of behaviors. However, you don't need to identify all of them. Instead, you need to identify behaviors that are relative to the goal of your system. Let's say you are writing a Computer Aided Design application that is used to design a house. One of the objects you'll need is a window. The application shows how the window looks when installed in the house. Therefore, you only need to include two behaviors: open the window and close the window. You don't need to include how the window behaves in a hurricane because the application doesn't simulate the structural behavior of a window.

Object-oriented programmers identify behaviors of an object by brainstorming. They begin by creating a two-column table, as shown in Table 7-2, and enter the name of each object in the first column. Next, they asked themselves, What does the object do in relation to the nature of the system that is being developed? Answers are behaviors and are listed in the second column.

Object	Behavior
Student	Register for course
	Drop course
	Take exam
	Select major
	Change major

Table 7-2   Identifying Behaviors of an Object

Table 7-2 contains just a few behaviors that are associated with a student. You can easily expand upon this list.

Describing Behaviors

Once you identify all the behaviors of an object that are needed by your application, you must describe each behavior in detail. The description of a behavior consists of data needed to perform the behavior, the steps to perform, and the data that is a result of performing the behavior, if there is any.

This should sound familiar to you. The description of a behavior is nearly identical to the definition of a function (method in Java). When you define a function, you need to identify the data needed to perform the function (arguments). You also need to define steps required to perform the function (body of the function), and you need to define the data that is returned after those steps are completed (return value).

There is a subtle difference between describing a behavior and defining a function. When describing a behavior, object-oriented programmers use a processing model diagram to illustrate the details of how the behavior is performed. The processing model diagram is then translated into *pseudo code*, which is a combination of English and a programming language that describes every detail of the processing model diagram. Pseudo code makes it easy for a programmer to encode the behavior into a program.

When a function is defined, the programmer uses C++, Java, or another programming language to define the details of how the function is to perform.

Processing Model

A processing model is shown in a diagram that describes how a behavior is performed. The diagram is built using symbols to represent aspects of the process. Figure 7-1 contains commonly used symbols that object-oriented programmers use to describe a processing model. You probably recognize these as flow chart symbols.

The processing model diagram is a flow chart that provides both an iconic description and textual description of a process. An *iconic* description is a picture of the process, whereas a *textual* description describes the process in words.

A symbol conveys a common step in the process, such as displaying a prompt on the screen or receiving input from the user of the system. Most systems have these common steps. Within the symbol is textual information that provides information specific to the system being described. For example, textual information in the display symbol describes the flavor of information that is displayed on the screen. Likewise, textual information in the input symbol describes the kind of information entered into the system by the user.

Any process can be described in detail by arranging these symbols into a processing flow that complements the processing that you want to describe. Let's say that you want to describe the process used by a student to enroll in a course. Here's how this process works.

First, the system prompts the student to enter the course number. After the student enters the course number, the system determines whether the course is open. If it is, then information about the student is enrolled in the course by placing the student's

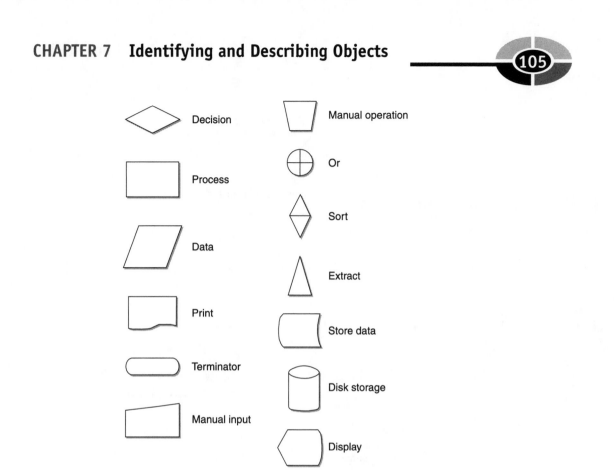

Figure 7-1   Symbols used to create a processing model

information in the appropriate database file. A conformation notice is then displayed on the screen. If the course is closed, a message is displayed on the screen informing the student that the course is closed.

Figure 7-2 shows the processing model diagram that describes this process. Notice that the diagram uses symbols rather than text to describe each step. The first step shows the display symbol followed by the input symbol. Anyone who reads the diagram is expected to know the meaning of those symbols because they are used in practically all processing model diagrams.

Within each symbol is text that provides information specific to each step. For example, the first step has the text "Prompt student for course number." This tells the reader of the processing model diagram the nature of text that is displayed on the screen during that step. You don't need to enter the complete text in the symbol, but just enough information to give the reader an idea what is being displayed at that moment in the process.

Figure 7-2 is just one of many processing model diagrams used to describe the details of an application. There could be hundreds of such diagrams that are connected together to describe the entire application. For example, the process shown in Figure 7-2 links to

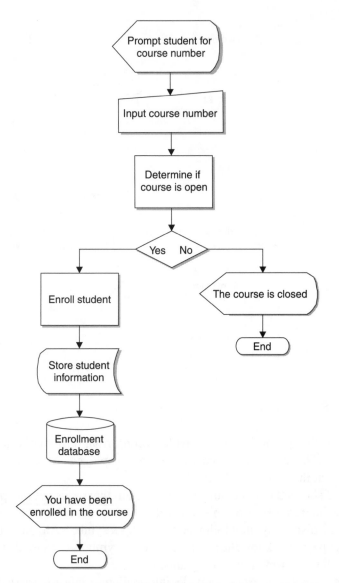

Figure 7-2 A processing model that illustrates how a student registers for a course

two other processes—a process to determine whether the course is open and another process that enrolls the student in the course. Each of these processes is represented in a rectangle in the diagram. The programmer must review the corresponding processing model diagram for each of these processes to determine the details on how they work.

Each process has a starting point and at least one termination point. There can be multiple termination points if the process takes different paths, depending on the results of evaluating a condition, as is the case in Figure 7-2. This process takes one of two paths, depending on whether the course is open or closed. Each path has its own termination point.

Each step of the process, as pictured by the symbols in the processing model diagram, must connect to a previous step and to the next step in the process, as illustrated in Figure 7-2. Arrows are used to connect each step and show the processing flow. Although the process in Figure 7-2 flows downward, processes can flow to previous steps. For example, a step might test a condition. If the condition is true, then other steps are processed afterward and the process returns to test the condition again. This process should sound familiar to you because it is the process used in a loop.

Pseudo Code

Some programmers begin coding an application by using information contained in the processing model diagram. Other programmers translate the processing model diagram into pseudo code. Previously in this chapter you learned that pseudo code is a combination of English words and programming language syntax that describe in words how a process works.

The following example is the pseudo code translation of the processing model diagram shown in Figure 7-2:

```
Prompt student to enter a course number
Read the course number
Determine if the course is open or closed
If the course is open
   Enroll the student
   Store the student's information into the course file
   Display enrollment confirmation on the screen.
else
   Display a message telling the student that the course is closed
end if
```

You can easily pick out English sentences from programming syntax and yet you don't have to be trained in programming to understand the process described in the pseudo code. Anyone can read the pseudo code under the process.

Pseudo code does more than describe a process. It also organizes steps into the logical sequence that the program must follow. This enables a programmer to focus on translating pseudo code into programming syntax, sometimes by simply replacing each step in pseudo code with the corresponding statement(s) of a programming language that is needed to perform the step.

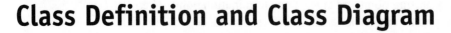
Class Definition and Class Diagram

Once a programmer identifies objects and their attributes and behaviors, the programmer then focuses on encoding these objects into the program by defining classes. Each class is an object, and members of the class are attributes and behaviors of the object. Throughout the first six chapters of this book, you learned how to define a class and member attributes and member behaviors of a class using Java and C++.

Some programmers create a class diagram before they set out to define classes for an application. A class diagram illustrates classes that are used in the application and also depicts the *class hierarchy*, which is like a genealogical chart that shows inheritance among classes.

A class diagram shows the class name, member attributes, member behaviors, and whether those member are defined in the public, protected, or private access specifier areas of the class.

Figure 7-3 shows five class diagrams and the class hierarchy. The class hierarchy begins with the Person class, which contains some attributes and behaviors related to every person. The attributes are defined within the protected access specifier area so that they can be accessed by member functions and by functions of classes that inherit the Person class.

Below the Person class in the class hierarchy is the Student class, which describes some attributes and behaviors found in a student. At the bottom of the class hierarchy are three classes: ContinuingEdStudent, UndergradStudent, and GradStudent. Each of these classes inherits the public and protected members of the Person class and of the Student class. In addition, each of these three classes defines attributes and member functions that are unique to their type of student.

It is a good practice to develop class diagrams and a class hierarchy for your application because programmers who develop the application and later maintain the application use this as a roadmap to understand the classes associated with the application. For example, a programmer who sets out to enhance the functionality of an application begins by reviewing class diagrams and the class hierarchy to determine if all or a portion of the functionality is already coded in an existing class. If so, the programmer can inherit the class and avoid having to write code that already exists.

Relationships Among Objects

Some objects have functional relationships rather than a hierarchical relationship. A functional relationship is one where two or more objects interact with each other but

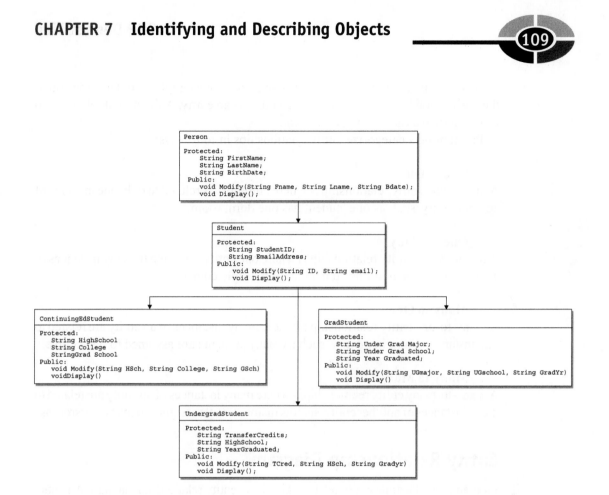

Figure 7-3   Class diagrams and the class hierarchy for various student classes

are not directly related to each other. A hierarchical relationship is one where objects are directly related through inheritance.

For example, a student fills out a registration form in order to register for a course. The student and the registration form are both objects that have a functional relationship, and neither is directly related through inheritance. The functional relationship is that a student uses a registration form to register for class.

Object-oriented programmers determine the functional relationship among objects in order to help them understand how objects work together to achieve the goal of the application.

An object is sometimes referred to as an *entity*. For example, a student is an entity, the registration form is an entity, and a course is an entity. A functional relationship is also known as an *entity relationship*.

Programmers categorize entity relationships in four ways:

One to One

A one-to-one entity relationship is where one entity is related to only one instance of another entity, such as one student has one dorm room.

One to Many

A one-to-many entity relationship is where one entity is related to many instances of another entity, such as one student takes multiple courses.

Many to One

A many-to-one entity relationship is where many instances of an entity are related to one instance of another entity, such as many students are assigned to one course.

Many to Many

A many-to-many entity relationship is where many instances of an entity are related to many instances of another entity, such as many students assigned to many classrooms.

Entity Relationship Diagram

Programmers illustrate entity relationships in an entity relationship diagram. An entity relationship diagram depicts a graphic representation of how one entity is associated with another entity.

An entity relationship diagram contains three components: entities, the functional relationship, and a ratio that indicates the type of relationship. Look at Figure 7-4 to see how these components are used.

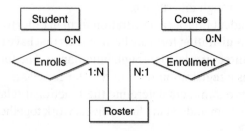

Figure 7-4 An entity relationship diagram of a student entity and a course entity

Figure 7-4 is an entity relationship between a student and a course. The functional relationship is that a student enrolls in a course, and a course has enrollment. Both of these functions result in a roster for the course. The roster is also an entity.

The type of a relationship is represented by a ratio. The student ratio 0:N means that a student can register for no courses or many courses. The N in the ratio implies any number. That is, a student can still be a student at the college without having to register for a course. The course ratio 0:N means that a course might have no students enrolled or many students enrolled. That is, the college can offer a course and no one enrolls in the course.

The ratio changes once a student registers for a course to reflect a change in relationship among the entities. The student ratio is now 1:N, meaning that the student registered for at least one course, but could register for many courses. Likewise, the course ratio is N:1, indicating that many students can enroll in one course.

Programmers use an entity relationship diagram to help in the design of their application so as to ensure that the application can handle all possible relationships. For example, the registration application must be able to handle a course without an enrollment and a course where any number of students can be enrolled.

Leveling Diagram

An object-oriented application can easily become complex and difficult to understand. Programmers simplify this complexity by using a leveling diagram, which depicts an application in layers, where the top level has the least amount of detail and is the easiest to understand. Subsequent levels have more detail and are usually the hardest to understand.

Each level illustrates entities and processes. As the programmer drills down into the leveling diagram, they learn more details about each process. Figure 7-5 shows the first level of a leveling diagram that depicts how the bursar collects tuition from students.

Rectangles are used to represent entities, which are Student and Bursar in this example. Circles represent processes, such as registration, tuition, and payment of tuition. Also, two parallel lines are used to signify a *data store,* which is simply a place where data is stored. This example has two data stores: one that stores student information and another that stores tuition information. Arrows are used to show a movement of data among entities, processes, and data stores.

Notice that each process is assigned a unique number. This number is used to connect the first level with lower levels of the leveling diagram. Take a look at Figure 7-6 and you'll see how this works.

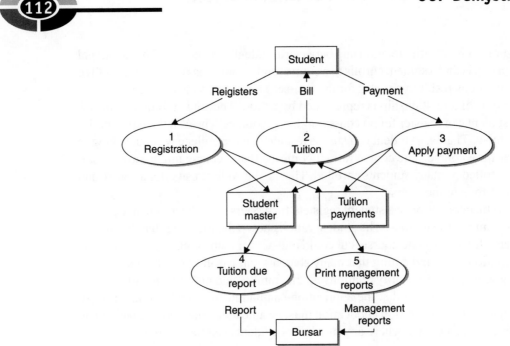

Figure 7-5   The first level of the leveling diagram shows all the processes involved in how the bursar collects tuition from students.

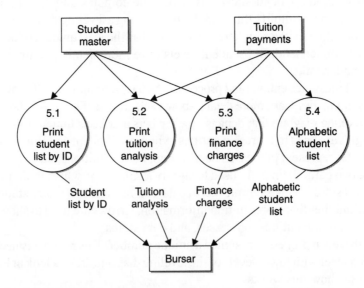

Figure 7-6   Level 2 of the leveling diagram shows details of the Print Management Reports process from Level 1.

Figure 7-6 is the second level of the level diagram and describes the Print Management Reports process shown on Level 1. The Print Management Reports process actually has many subprocesses—one for each report. The second level shows these processes. Notice that each of the subprocesses is assigned a unique number. The number begins with corresponding number of the process shown on Level 1. Each of these subprocesses begins with 5, which is the number of the Print Management Reports process in Level 1.

The subprocess number contains a decimal followed by another number, which represents the subprocess in Level 2. For example, Print Student List By ID is the first subprocess on Level 2 and therefore is numbered 5.1. The number 5 links this subprocess to a process on Level 1, and the number 1 indicates this is the first subprocess on Level 2.

The same progression is used for subsequent levels. For example, you would look in Level 3 at process 5.1.1 to learn the details of the process used to print the student list by ID.

Quiz

1. What is the difference between an attribute and data?

2. What is the purpose of using a leveling diagram?

3. What is an entity?

4. What is the purpose of using an entity relationship diagram?

5. What does 0:N mean?

6. What is the purpose of decomposing an attribute?

7. What is a processing model?

8. What is pseudo code?

9. What is a class diagram?

10. What is a many-to-one relationship?

8

Real-World Modeling

Remember back during your grammar school days when you tried to shape a hunk of modeling clay into your favorite car? No matter how much you poked, pulled, and pounded, the clay never resembled an automobile. And yet designers for auto manufacturers poke, pull, and pound the same clay as you, but are able to transform the hunk of clay into a work of art that eventually drives onto the showroom floor. Auto designers have the know-how to model a real-world automobile out of clay. The same can be said about professional object-oriented programmers. They have the skills to apply object-oriented programming theory to model real-world objects in a program. You'll learn those skills in this chapter.

Theory vs. the Real World

Experienced object-oriented programmers soon realize after learning their trade that the real world isn't as perfect as the examples used to explain the concepts of object-oriented programming. Somehow the real world cannot always be organized into clearly defined objects that can be represented by classes in an application.

Programmers have to be adept at applying object-oriented programming theory where it makes sense without unnecessarily complicating the coding in an application. They also have to be clever to know when *not* to use object-oriented programming in an application.

We'll explore the realities of using object-oriented programming to model the real world throughout this chapter and in doing so we'll illustrate common problems and how experienced programmers overcome them.

From Simple Beginnings

Some programmers believe the popularity of object-oriented programming was seeded by the development of graphical user interfaces (GUIs) because a GUI is composed of objects such as buttons, radio buttons, list boxes, and other familiar graphics. Each object is encapsulated with data and behaviors.

For example, the push button object encapsulates data such as height, width, color, text, and screen position. It also encapsulates behaviors such as the actions that occur when the cursor is placed over the button, when the cursor moves away from the button, and when the button is clicked.

A GUI screen is built by selecting objects from a toolbox and placing them on the screen. The screen inherits all the data and behaviors of an object. The GUI is one of the successful implementations of object-oriented programming theory because GUI objects fit the object-oriented programming model.

Object-Oriented vs. Procedural Languages

Some programmers feel that object-oriented programming theory must be tempered with the needs of real-world applications by combining object-oriented techniques and procedural programming techniques to create a natural, easy-to-use and maintainable application.

You might be wondering what the differences are between these two programming techniques. We'll turn to English language syntax to describe the difference. Object-oriented programming groups things around nouns, such as *customer* and *invoice*, which you'll recognize as objects.

In contrast, procedural programming groups things around verbs. A verb in the real world is a task. This means the focus of a procedural programmer is on tasks that are performed by the application, whereas an object-oriented programmer focuses on an object, its data, and its behaviors.

Procedural programmers also use nouns (such as customer and invoice), too, but they are described in a database and not in the application code. For example, the task of searching for an invoice stored in a database is separate from the invoice itself. This means you don't need to create an object called *invoice* in order to search for an invoice. In object-oriented program, you need to create an invoice object because the search behavior is encapsulated in the invoice object.

Behavior Problems

Some programmers feel the basic premise that objects have behaviors isn't always true in the real world. It works well for GUI objects, but some real-world objects can be acted upon by behaviors of other objects or behaviors that are not associated with any object.

Take submitting an order form for processing as an example. Is this task associated with a sales representative object? How about a customer who directly places the order without the assistance of a sales representative? Maybe this is a standalone process that isn't associated directly with an object.

The real world doesn't necessarily restrict a task to an object, although object-oriented programming theory does require that a task be associated with an object. One of the challenges of applying object-oriented programming techniques is to know when to hold true to object-oriented programming theory and when to deviate from the theory to address real-world problems that cannot be handled efficiently using object-oriented programming techniques.

Object-oriented programming uses multilevel inheritance to avoid redundancy, but there is redundancy in the real world. For example, employees and customers both have contact information. An object-oriented programming approach might be to create an object called *contact information* that is inherited by objects called *employee* and *customer*. In the real world, contact information is directly related with an employee and customer without any inheritance.

Simulation May Not Be the Objective

Another underlying premise of object-oriented programming is that object-oriented programming is well-suited to simulate real-world objects in a computer application. This is true; however, many business applications do not simulate real-world business situations. A *simulation* is a technique that re-creates the real world in a computer in order to study how the real world works and how to improve a real-world process. In contrast, the purpose of a business application is to achieve a business objective using the best possible means. The reality is that simulating the real world does not necessarily use the best possible means to achieve a business objective.

Some programmers use airplanes and flying to illustrate the difference between simulating real life and achieving an objective using efficient means. Prior to the airplane, real-world flight was achieved by flapping wings. Therefore, if we set out to simulate flight, airplanes would have flapping wings—and probably never would have gotten off the ground. Simulation, therefore, isn't a means to achieve the goal of flight.

On the surface, modeling the real world using object-oriented programming seems like a good way to develop a business application that simulates real-world business situations. However, simulation may not be the true objective of the application. Instead, the application's goal is to get something done efficiently. Blindly adhering to object-oriented programming design philosophies may not produce the best business application because object-oriented programming may not lend itself to designing an application that takes advantage of the strengths of computers.

Although we look at the real world in terms of objects, that view sometimes doesn't provide us with the flexibility needed to provide the best possible flow of a business application. Some programmers who strictly apply object-oriented programming design techniques to a business application may gloss over simplicity and efficiency in order to fit the theoretical design requirements. This results in failure to achieve the goal of the business application.

The objective of every programmer is to develop an application that improves the processing flow and not simply to mirror the real world. It doesn't make sense for an application to simulate every step in a manual process when the process can be reduced to fewer steps when performed by a computer.

Internal Model and External Model

You must strike a balance when using object-oriented programming to develop an application. The desire to simulate the real world by creating objects that have data and behaviors should not overshadow the need to develop an application that is efficient and improves the business process.

Programmers strike this balance by developing two models: the internal model and the external model. The internal model describes how an application works behind the scenes. The external model describes how a person interacts with the application.

In a perfect world, a programmer develops an application where both the internal and external models mirror real-world objects. For example, an order form is an object used to record and process a customer order. Ideally, the order form that appears on the screen should resemble the paper order form, thus enabling the user to relate the computerized order form to the real-world order form. Likewise, behind the scenes an order form object is created and is used to process order information.

In reality, the programmer probably uses the order form as the external model for an application, but might decide not to create an order form object for the internal model because it may not be the most efficient way to manage and process an order.

You should address the internal model and external model independently whenever you develop an application. Don't assume that you have to use object-oriented programming concepts to address every aspect of an application. Instead, apply those concepts that make sense for your application.

Hierarchical Problems

You won't be able to use hierarchical classification to describe every real-life object because the real world doesn't work that way. You might find yourself going to great lengths to develop a complex structure of objects in order to simulate the real world, when in reality you don't require such sophistication to achieve the business objective. Don't develop an object-oriented application in a vacuum. Always keep your sights on the objective of the application.

Sometimes you might discover that procedural and relational design techniques are much better suited for a portion of your application than object-oriented design. Procedural design focuses on tasks, which some programmers refer to as the "verb approach" because a procedure is an action. Relational design refers to application data stored in a relational database. Some programmers refer to this as the "noun approach" because, collectively, data describes a person, place, or thing.

One of the several attractions of a hierarchical solution is that we envision reuse of code in the base or super classes. Although this is always a key goal for professional developers, sometimes it just doesn't work. For example, we have discussed student classes extensively throughout this book. But, for all our design of these classes, they have no use if we are next asked to design an application to track stock quotes.

Although hierarchical design is always desirable, don't spend an inordinate amount of time trying to design systems solely for the purpose of the design. Use your common sense, run through several "what if" scenarios to see how things will work, and try to identify your reusable code and objects.

You will typically find that your code reuse and hierarchy fall into three categories: objects that are very reusable across different applications (such as a string class or stream hierarchy), objects that are reusable within a particular set of programs (such as our student class and hierarchy for academic institution programs), and objects that simply will never be reused again, anywhere.

Task Oriented, Not Object Oriented

A staple of object-oriented programming is to encapsulate tasks within a real-world object. However, sometimes this doesn't make sense because a task is associated with many objects instead of one object.

You'll run into this problem from time to time when developing an object-oriented program. Some programmers address this situation by creating a super class that defines the common task and then have objects that are associated with the task inherit the super class. Those subclasses can then call the task as required by the application.

Although this approach adheres to the principles of object-oriented programming, it can result in an overly complex application, especially if the only purpose of the super class is to facilitate the common task.

Professional programmers apply principles of object-oriented programming with a grain of common sense. Simplicity overrules the need to strictly adhere to object-oriented programming standards. They don't build classes simply to adhere to standards when a simpler alternative is available.

If there is a task that is associated with several classes, a programmer might consider defining a function that isn't a member of a class to handle the task. The function can be designed to use a variety of objects as required by the application. Those objects can be passed as parameters to the function.

Let's use the task of registering a student for a class as an example. Several approaches can be taken to implement the registration processing in an application. For example, you can define a separate class for each type of student (undergraduate, graduate, postgraduate, continuing education) and then define a registration member function for each class.

The registration process is basically the same for all students; therefore, it might not make sense to have several definitions of the same function. Another alternative is to define a super class that contains the definition of the registration function. Each type of student class then can inherit the super class and gain access to the registration function.

The super class approach is ideal if there are other commonalities among each type of student class. Common data and functions can be defined in one place—in the super class. This simplifies maintenance of the application.

Suppose the registration function is the only thing common among the types of student classes. Does it make sense to create a new super class for the sole purpose of defining the registration process? Some programmers will say yes, because doing so conforms to object-oriented programming conventions. Other programmers will disagree because doing so unnecessarily adds to the complexity of the application.

A more desirable alternative is to define a registration function that isn't a member of a class. The registration function can be designed to register any type of student.

Self-Contained Data vs. Wide Source of Data

Sometimes the real world isn't built from well-defined objects, although object-oriented programming theory assumes this to be the case. This is apparent in business applications where data required by a process might come from multiple objects rather than encapsulated into one object.

A typical example of this is the month-end processing common to nearly all businesses. A month-end process summarizes the state of the business that occurs during the month. Data used for month-end processes typically comes from a variety of objects associated with multiple systems throughout the company.

For example, month-end processing summarizes customer account information, order information, and inventory information. Each of these is likely generated by an accounting system, transaction system, and inventory system. And within each of these systems is an assortment of objects, such as customer, product, and order.

It is difficult to associate the month-end process with a single object because no one object involved in the monthly summary process owns this process. A solution might be to define another object for the sole purpose of defining the month-end process. However, doing so unnecessarily complicates the application.

Therefore, modeling a real-world business using object-oriented programming isn't as straightforward as you might believe. There will be situations when the real world doesn't fit the theoretical object-oriented programming model, and you'll need to be less rigid in applying object-oriented programming theory to your application.

The World in Discrete Pieces

Developing a real-world object-oriented application is more challenging than the exercises used to explain the concepts of object-oriented programming. This is because only real-world objects that lend themselves to a class definition are used in those exercises.

Many instructors demonstrate the concept of object-oriented programming by using the example of an airplane or automobile, where the engine, wheels, and other components are objects contained by the airplane or automobile. These real-world objects fit nicely into an object definition. However, not all real-world objects do—a factor that isn't mentioned in many books on object-oriented programming.

Do We Think in Objects?

Some programmers question whether we really view the real world as objects and feel that we look at things as tasks and data rather than as objects. For example, when your house is hot, you probably think about lowering the temperature by turning on the air conditioner or by opening a window. You don't think air condition, turn on, or window, open, which is the logic used if you thought about objects first and then the behaviors associated with those objects.

This subtle difference can become a mental roadblock for programmers who model the real world in a computer application because programmers tend to mimic the way we look at the real world. Programmers have to alter their natural thinking process in order to model the real world.

OOP and Data

Data is another mental stumbling block when modeling the real world using object-oriented programming. Data is encapsulated in an object according to object-oriented programming theory. There are few data elements in an application that aren't encapsulated with an object.

The difficulty occurs when storing data in a database. Although there are object-oriented databases, many programmers use one of the popular relational databases, such as Oracle, DB2, or Sybase, as data storage for their applications.

A relational database doesn't store objects; it stores *data*. This means the programmer must write routines that extract encapsulated data in a form where data can be stored in a relational database. Likewise, data retrieved from a relational database must be restructured so that data can be encapsulated into one or more objects in the application.

Sometimes programmers build conversion routines into the member functions of an object that are used to extract and restructure data to and from a relational database. Other times programmers develop middleware software that sits between the application and the relational database. Middleware software contains conversion routines that interact with both the object-oriented application and the relational database.

A conversion routine maps fields to the data members of objects, and it maps data members of objects to the fields of a relational database. This is a time-consuming process that is required only because data is encapsulated in an object. Some programmers feel conversion routines unnecessarily complicate an application—these routines are required only because the application is written using an object-oriented programming language and not because they are a requirement of the application.

Real-World Hierarchy

Another staple of object-oriented programming is that the real world is organized into objects, and objects are associated with other objects in a hierarchy. In reality, objects found in the real world form one of two kinds of hierarchies: a static hierarchy or a dynamic hierarchy.

Objects in a static hierarchy don't change or change very little over a long time period. Most things in nature are objects that have a static hierarchy. These are also the same objects used to describe the concepts of object-oriented programming.

An object in a dynamic hierarchy frequently changes its relationship with other objects in the hierarchy. Objects used in business applications typically have a dynamic hierarchy. In fact, some business objects tend to have a matrix hierarchy that consists of cross-relationships. You've probably seen this in organizations for which you've worked where some workers (objects) report directly to one boss and have a cross-reporting relationship to one or more other bosses. Then the relationship changes when a reorganization occurs within the firm.

Relationships among nearly every object used to model an organization are fluid and therefore don't lend themselves to the nicely organized concepts defined in object-oriented programming.

A dynamic hierarchy of objects used to model an organization can become troublesome to programmers who must apply object-oriented theory in order to model the organization within an application. Programmers might find themselves trying to fit an octagonal peg into a round hole. The peg is almost round, but not round enough to meet the definition of the circle.

The Morphing of a Hierarchy

Whenever a programmer encounters a conflict between object-oriented programming theory and the real world, they have a tendency to carve the real world to adhere to object-oriented programming theory. What results is the morphing of the hierarchy of the real world when the real world is modeled in an application.

Morphing is evident when a real-world object is defined as a subobject. A *subobject* is a division of a real-world object. An object has an "is a" relationship with a super class. For example, a surfboard is a vehicle. A subobject might have an "is almost" relationship with a super class, such as a tabletop is a vehicle when it is used as a surfboard.

The issue for a programmer is how to handle all the variations that exist in the real world that are almost like well-defined objects. *Polymorphism* is a concept many programmers use to address this issue. Previously in this book you learned that polymorphism enables a programmer to use the same name for slightly different behaviors by changing the argument list to specify which variation of the behavior to use in the application.

At first glance, polymorphism seems to address this issue, but what constitutes slightly different behavior? Can a behavior that varies by 25 percent from the original behavior be considered a slight difference? If so, then polymorphism can be applied. If not, then a new member function needs to be defined.

The real world has many "is almost" objects that behave similarly to another behavior, but the degree of the similarity falls within a very wide range. The programmer must decide how similar a behavior is to another behavior and be careful not to morph the original behavior too much; otherwise, application programmers won't recognize the member function.

Let's say that an ordering system has multiple ways to retrieve an order. The order is an object that has member functions an application programmer can use to retrieve an order. If there are 30 ways to retrieve an order, then there could be 30 versions of the function that retrieves an order. Is it feasible for the application programmer to learn all 30 versions of the function? It might be more efficient to define more functions with fewer versions, where each function focuses on a set of ways to retrieve an order.

"Is a" Problems

As you learned in earlier chapters, a programmer determines whether an object should inherit another object if it passes the "is a" test. The "is a" test asks the question, Is object A an object B? If so, then object A can inherit object B. For example, is a graduate student a student? If so, then the graduate student object can inherit the student object. If not, then the graduate student object cannot inherit the student object.

The "is a" test isn't as flexible as a "has a" relationship, and some real-world objects don't have an "is a" relationship with other objects but do have a "has a" relationship with them. This is true in business applications where there is a dynamic hierarchy among objects.

It's also worth noting that although inheritance and containment define two classes that are very closely related somehow—a truck "is a" vehicle, and a vehicle "has a(n)" engine—some objects aren't so closely related, but still need to interact with other objects. We are referring to *collaboration*, which is described in more detail in the section titled "Common Procedures."

Collaboration is a means to define how objects will work together, without having to define them in terms of inheritance or containment.

The Real-World Challenges of Object-Oriented Programming

Now that you understand many of the challenges you'll face applying object-oriented programming theory in real-world situations, let's take a closer look at common problems and how the pros resolve them. Here's what we'll explore:

- Data storage
- Common procedures
- Defining objects
- Hierarchy

Data Storage

Data storage is a common challenge when designing an object-oriented program because there is a philosophical conflict between the way many organizations store data and object-oriented programming design, as you learned in this chapter.

Organizations use a relational database to store data, which coincides with the procedural style of programming. Objects defined in object-oriented programming don't lend themselves easily to a relational database model because a relational database is not suited for storing objects. An object-oriented database is designed to store objects; however, typically organizations don't use an object-oriented database.

Your problem is how to resolve this conflict when writing an object-oriented program that requires data storage. Professional programmers address this issue by writing functions that translate data members of objects to a relational database model, and vice versa.

To do this requires four functions: insert(), search(), modify(), and delete(). The insert() function converts data members of objects defined by your application into data elements, and it organizes the data elements into one or more records required by the corresponding relational database. The insert() function also contains the SQL query that places these records into the database.

The search() function retrieves one or more records from the relational database. It does this by using a query to find the search criteria for the record and then converting the returning record into the data members of a corresponding object within the application. The object is then typically displayed on the screen.

The `search()` function is used in conjunction with the `modify()` and `delete()` functions. After the desired data is displayed, the user of the application causes the `modify()` or `delete()` function to be executed. The `modify()` function enables the user to change the data of an object that was retrieved from the database. It then converts the data members of the object to its corresponding record and then updates the record in the relational database. The `delete()` function removes the record from the database.

Common Procedures

Previously in this chapter, you learned how object-oriented programming and the real world don't always compliment each other. The real world cannot always be nicely organized into discrete objects. You should expect to run into conflicts between how the real world works and object-oriented programming philosophy.

A common conflict occurs with procedures. Procedures should be encapsulated within an object definition. Yet there are times when a procedure crosses the boundary of two or more objects. It doesn't make sense to encapsulate into any one object. This situation leaves programmers in a dilemma of where to define the procedure in the application.

According to the spirit of object-oriented programming, the programmers should define an object that encapsulates the procedure and then have other objects inherit it. In this way, the procedure is available to multiple objects without having to repeat the procedure.

Although this approach is totally acceptable, it can lead to overly complex code that contains too many objects for an application programmer to learn and remember. This is especially true if there are many situations within the application where procedures can be associated with more than one object.

Here's what to do when you encounter this conflict. Balance the need to adhere to object-oriented design philosophy and the need for an uncomplicated application. If the sole purpose of defining an object is to accommodate a procedure, then consider defining the procedure as a stand-alone procedure rather than defining another object. A stand-alone procedure is acceptable in an object-oriented program if it makes sense to the application.

On the other hand, if the procedure can be encapsulated in an object that contains other procedures that are common across my objects, then define a new object. It makes sense to do so because the object can be used to accommodate more than one procedure.

Defining Objects

Identifying objects in the real world seems intuitive, but it can become challenging when you actually have to define objects for your application because some real-world things could be interpreted as two or more objects.

Take a student as an example. A student is an obvious object. However, there is more than one kind of student. There are undergraduate students, graduate students, postgraduate students, and continuing education students. Each kind of student can be its own object. Alternatively, student can be the object, and attributes of student could describe the kind of student.

You'll run into similar conflicts when developing an object-oriented application. Programmers resolve such conflicts by developing a "keep it simple" philosophy. Avoid creating too many objects in an application. Don't divide an object into many objects unless there is a compelling reason to do so. Instead, define one object and use attributes and member procedures to make the distinction among the different kinds of objects.

Throughout the examples in this book we've defined objects for each kind of student because we used these objects to illustrate various features of object-oriented programming. However, baring any unique requirement of an application, it makes sense to define one object called student and then define attributes and member procedures to distinguish each kind of student.

In general, the fewer objects that are defined in application, the easier it will be for programmers to understand and maintain the code of an application. Some programmers only define objects that directly correspond to major entities of a real-world process, such as a customer, product, order form, invoice, and sales representative. They avoid defining objects for the sake of adhering to strict object-oriented design philosophy because doing so has a tendency to make an application overly and unnecessarily complex.

Hierarchy

There is a tendency for programmers who recently discover the power of object-oriented programming to go wild creating a complex hierarchy for their applications and lose track of the application's goal. In doing so they create multilevel inheritance that is technically sound, but a challenge to maintain.

Avoid creating unnecessary inheritance, especially inheritance that involves more than three levels. Most real-world applications will be operational for years and maintained and enhanced by a series of programmers who need to focus on upgrading the code rather than learning a complex trail of inheritance within the application.

As a general rule, keep the hierarchy of your application to no more than three levels of inheritance, unless additional levels have a direct, positive impact on achieving the objective of the application. If the additional levels won't materially improve the application, then don't implement those levels in your program.

The Computer World vs. the Real World

Another interesting aspect to note about object-oriented programming is that while we try our best to mimic things in the real world, some things don't have exact physical counterparts in the real world. Some things are conceptual, or may at first be considered too simple to be broken down into real-world objects.

For example, a sorting algorithm or technique isn't a real world "thing" but rather more a method. A linked list also isn't a real-world thing, though we might see examples of them or use them programmatically on a daily basis. With a bit of work, we can start to imagine how these things might work in the real world, but it would be in a way that nobody actually does things.

Let's take the linked list example a step further: A linked list is a collection of "nodes." Each node contains a reference (or pointer) to the next node as well as some additional data we wish to manage. Now, we would never actually have a linked list node in the real world, but we can picture how one might work. Let's imagine we have a blank fixed-page notebook, where each page contains only a preprinted page number, as in Figure 8-1.

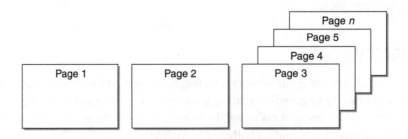

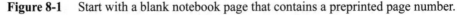

Figure 8-1   Start with a blank notebook page that contains a preprinted page number.

We want to keep track of a person's name and phone number, ordered by their name. Now, in a linked list, the *data* portion would be the person's name and number; this is what we really are interested in working with. The linked list also has a reference to the next item in the list, which makes everything work as desired. In our example now, the "reference" is actually another page number representing the next person, but in a programming language it might be an object reference, pointer, or index (into an array).

Let's imagine that our first person to add is Eric Carruthers. We would write down on the first page his name, because he is the first person. Because no other people exists after him, we would also write down a "Next" and "Previous" value of 0, meaning there are no more people before or after him. Our book now looks like Figure 8-2.

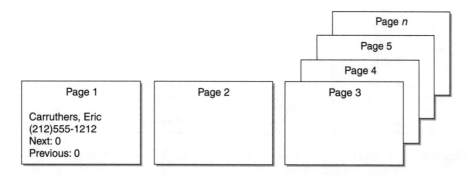

Figure 8-2   After entering Eric Carruthers on the page, we would note that there isn't a next or previous page because Eric Carruthers is the only name in the book.

Next, Rene Winston is added to our book. We write her name on page 2, and we set her Previous value to 1, meaning "go to page 1 for the person before." We write 0 for the Next value on her page, as we did for Eric, but we also modify Eric's page so that Next now indicates page 2. Figure 8-3 shows how the book looks now.

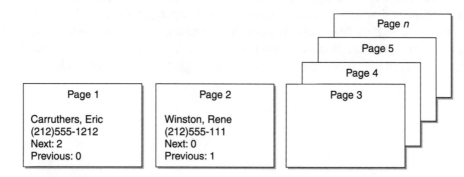

Figure 8-3   When we add Rene Winston to the book, we modify Eric's page by changing Next from 0 to 2.

Finally, we add Harry Gee. Because our notebook isn't a loose-leaf binder, we can't just reshuffle pages. Instead, we write his name on page 3. We have all our data, but we still need to make the book "work," so we write down page 2 as Harry's Next value, and page 1 as Harry's Previous value. We also need to modify Eric Carruthers' record and change his Next value to page 3, and we need to change Rene Winston's record so that her Previous value is page 3. The end result is shown in Figure 8-4.

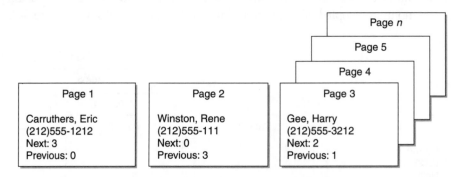

Figure 8-4   When Harry Gee is entered into the book, we modify previous pages to reflect the new addition.

As you can see from this example, a real-world implementation of a linked list would not be a practical solution. In order to find a person, you would have to start at the first page and read it to find out where the page for the next person (alphabetically) is, and keep doing that until you find the person you want. However, in computer terms, this is a very straightforward and rapid process (because a computer is performing the task, not a human).

If you find yourself designing classes and find out that the system needs some sort of mechanism that doesn't have a real-world counterpart, don't panic. Just switch to "computer world" mode and design the objects to make them work as needed. Note that in this section we have discussed something called a *linked list*, which, due to the fact that we can call it a "thing" means there's a good chance we can create a class for it.

Quiz

1. How is data stored in a typical object-oriented application?

2. How are approaches to programming analogous to nouns and verbs?

3. What prevents some business applications from being modeled using object-oriented programming?

4. What is a dynamic hierarchy?

5. What is a static hierarchy?

6. How can a hierarchy be morphed?

7. Do we look at the real world as objects?

8. Explain the potential conflict between the simplicity of an application and adherence to object-oriented programming theory.

9. Is the objective of an object-oriented program to simulate the real world?

10. What is the difference between an internal model and an external model?

Collaboration

Try telling your instructor on the next computer programming assignment that building a computer program is a collaborative effort. You may get a few extra-credit points for being observant, but it is unlikely that you'll be allowed to collaborate with your friends to complete the assignment. Although collaboration is frowned upon in the classroom, it is a cornerstone of software development. Collaboration occurs when programmers of different skills join forces to build an application. Collaboration also occurs in software design when components collaborate to form an industrial-strength application. In this chapter, you'll learn how to design components so they collaborate in making a real-world application.

What Is Collaboration?

Collaboration occurs when two or more things work together or cooperate with each other in order to achieve a common goal. Collaboration is used in a military operation where branches of different military services join forces to achieve a strategic objective. Accounting, manufacturing, marketing, distribution, sales, and other areas of a typical corporation collaborate to satisfy customer needs and make a profit for the business. Even different kinds of businesses, such as bankers, manufacturers, distributors, and retailers, work with each other to build, sell, and deliver products that customers demand.

Processes are at the center of nearly all collaboration. A *process* is a collection of tasks that is identified by a name and performed whenever the process executes. Think of a process as a function or a method in a program. For example, taking a final examination is a process and consists of a relatively standard set of tasks.

Typically a process collaborates with other related but different processes to achieve an objective. Each process in a collaboration is unable to achieve the objective by itself and therefore forms an interdependency among collaborative processes in order to achieve the objective.

For example, an objective of your instructor is to determine whether you pass the course. To do this, the instructor uses a collaborative collection of processes to assess how much of the material presented in class you learned. These processes consist of homework assignments, class participation, quizzes, a midterm examination, a final examination, and possibly a course project. Individually, each process gives a glimpse of what you know but is not sufficient to determine whether you have enough knowledge to pass the course. However, collectively, these processes give your instructor and you a measure of your knowledge.

Inside a Process

Each process performs a unique set of tasks. Some programmers say that a process does one thing very well. By combining processes, a programmer is able to create an application that does many things very well.

Similar to a function and method, a process performs one or more tasks depending on the tasks defined in the process. A process may require input necessary for processing, although not all processes require input. Likewise, a process may have output, but all processing doesn't require output.

Processes collaborate in two ways. Each process can interact with another, or each process can execute independently of other processes. Interaction between processes occurs when the output of a process becomes the input for another process. This exchange of information is the way in which both processes collaborate with each other. The exchange is similar to passing one or more parameters to a function or method.

An example of this is when a student registers for a course. Registration is a process. The output of the registration process becomes input to the tuition process. The tuition process receives the student's ID, number of credits attempted, and the course number, among other information. The tuition process then performs the tasks necessary to generate the tuition bill, which is the output of the tuition process.

Not all processes collaborate directly with each other. Some collaboration occurs by simply executing processes in a sequence. This happens when your instructor determines whether you pass your course. Homework, quizzes, midterm exam, final exam, and course project are all processes that collaboratively tell the instructor whether you learned the material presented in the course. Each process executes independent of other processes but must execute in the proper sequence in order to determine whether you pass.

OOP Collaboration

Sharing of processes is a hallmark of how real-world objects collaborate. A student cannot attend class unless the student enters into collaboration with the registrar to enroll in a course. Therefore, the student is said to share the process performed by the registrar needed to enroll students into courses.

In object-oriented programming, collaboration occurs among objects that mimic real-world objects inside an application. Throughout this book, you've learned that an object is a person, place, or thing that has attributes and behaviors. As you'll recall, an attribute is data, and a behavior is a process referred to as a *function* or *method,* depending on the object-oriented programming language being used to develop the application.

Let's see how collaboration works by continuing the course registration example we've used throughout this book. Here is the Student class we discussed extensively in other chapters:

```
class Student
{
   protected:
      int m_Graduation, m_ID;
      char m_First[16], m_Last[16];
   public:
      virtual void Display()
         {
            cout << "ID: " << m_ID << endl;
            cout << "First: " << m_First << endl;
            cout << "Last: " << m_Last << endl;
            cout << "Graduation: " << m_Graduation << endl;
         }
      void Modify( int ID, char First[], char Last[],
         int Graduation )
         {
```

```
            m_ID = ID;
            strcpy( m_First, First );
            strcpy( m_Last, Last );
            m_Graduation = Graduation;
        }
        Student()
        {
            m_ID = m_Graduation = 0;
            m_First[0] = m_Last[0] = '\0';
        }
int GetID() cons
        {
            return( m_ID );
        }
};
```

Besides the Student class, we'll also require another class to represent a course within the application. We'll call this class Course. The Course class contains all the information about a specific course, such as the course name, the course ID, and the instructor for the course, as shown in the following class definition. A course, however, does not contain students. Students are enrolled and attend a course, but are not actually "inside" the course.

```
class Course
{
    protected:
        char m_Name[50];
        int m_ID;
    public:
        Course()
        {
            m_Name[0] = '\0';
            m_ID = 0;
        }
        virtual void Display ()
        {
            cout << "Course Name: " << m_Name << endl;
            cout << "Course ID: " << m_ID << endl;
        }
        virtual void Modify( const char* Name, int ID )
        {
            strcpy( m_Name, Name );
            m_ID = ID;
        }
```

```
    int GetID() const
    {
        return( m_ID );
    }
};
```

As you've probably realized, something is missing from the `Student` class and the `Course` class. The `Student` class makes no reference to courses being taken by a student. Likewise, the `Course` class makes no reference to students who are taking the course. Therefore, there isn't any way for a student to register for a course and for a course to produce a roster of students who are taking the course.

We fill this gap by defining another class that links students with courses. We'll call this the `LinkCourseStudent` class. Its definition is next. Notice that the `LinkCourseStudent` class relates one student to one course rather than list all students registered for a particular course. We do this because we'll be declaring an array of instances of the `LinkCourseStudent` class. Each array is a course, and elements of each array are students enrolled in the course. The array is declared in the `Enrollments` class, which is described here:

```
class LinkCourseStudent
{
    protected:
        int m_StudentID, m_CourseID;
        char m_Grade;
    public:
        LinkCourseStudent()
        {
            m_StudentID = m_CourseID = 0;
            m_Grade = '\0';
        }
        virtual void Modify( int StudentID, int CourseID,
            char Grade='\0' )
        {
            m_StudentID = StudentID;
            m_CourseID = CourseID;
            m_Grade = Grade;
        }
        virtual void Display()
        {
            if( m_Grade != '\0' )
                cout << "Grade: " << m_Grade << endl;
            else
                cout << "Grade not assigned" << endl;
        }
```

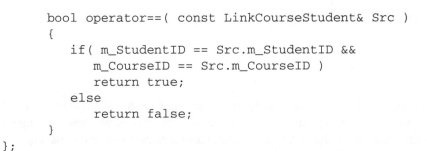

```
bool operator==( const LinkCourseStudent& Src )
{
    if( m_StudentID == Src.m_StudentID &&
        m_CourseID == Src.m_CourseID )
        return true;
    else
        return false;
}
};
```

You will see in the definition of the LinkCourseStudent class that it contains three attributes or data members: a Student ID, a Course ID, and a grade. Therefore, one LinkCourseStudent object can be used to link one student to one course. It also contains the student's grade if available. In database terms, this would be referred to as a *join* or *link* table, which essentially permits a many-to-many relationship between students and courses (that is, many students to a course, and many courses to a student).

The Display method of the LinkCourseStudent class only displays the grade for the given student in the given course. The student's name could be printed using the Student class's Display method, and the course name could be printed using the Course class's Display method.

The Enrollments class is an array of all LinkCourseStudent objects. As a design issue, we could have stated that either the Course class maintains its own enrollments for its students or that the Student class maintains its own enrollments of classes. However, in keeping with a typical database design, where the links between all Student objects and all Course objects is maintained in a separate table, we will use the Enrollments class, shown here, to manage the link between students and courses:

```
class Enrollments
{
    protected:
        vector< LinkCourseStudent > m_Links;
    public:
        bool Find( const Student& S, const Course& C )
        {
            return Find( S.GetID(), C.GetID() );
        }
        bool Find( int sID, int cID )
        {
            bool isRegistered = false;
            LinkCourseStudent Tmp;
            Tmp.Modify( sID, cID );
```

```
        for( int i=0; i < m_Links.size(); i++ )
        {
           if( Tmp == m_Links[i] )
           {
               isRegistered = true;
               break;
           }
        }
        return( isRegistered );
    }
    bool Register( const Student& S, const Course& C )
    {
        if( Find( S, C ) )
            return( false );
        LinkCourseStudent Tmp;
        Tmp.Modify( S.GetID(), C.GetID() );
        m_Links.push_back( Tmp );
        return( true );
    }
};
```

The last class we'll need is the `Registrar` class. The `Registrar` class is the catalyst that enables the student to register for a course and for the course to develop a roster. Here is the `Registrar` class definition:

```
class Registrar
{
   protected:
      // 'vector' is an array-type collection class
      vector< Course > m_Courses;
      vector< Student > m_Students;
      Enrollments m_Enrollments;
   public:
      void AddCourse( const char* Name, int ID )
      {
         Course aCourse;
         aCourse.Modify( Name, ID );
         m_Courses.push_back( aCourse );
      }
      void AddStudent( int ID, char First[], char Last[],
            int Graduation )
      {
         Student aStudent;
         aStudent.Modify( ID, First, Last, Graduation );
```

```
        m_Students.push_back( aStudent );
    }
    Course GetCourse( int ID )
    {
        for( int i=0; i < m_Courses.size(); i++ )
            if( m_Courses[i].GetID() == ID )
                return( m_Courses[i] );
        return( Course() );
    }
    Student GetStudent( int ID )
    {
        for( int i=0; i < m_Students.size(); i++ )
            if( m_Students[i].GetID() == ID )
                return( m_Students[i] );
            return( Student() );
    }
    bool Register( int StudentID, int CourseID )
    {
        int TheStudent, TheCourse;
        for( TheStudent = 0; TheStudent < m_Students.size();
                TheStudent++ )
            if( StudentID == m_Students[TheStudent].GetID() )
                break;
        for( TheCourse = 0; TheCourse < m_Courses.size();
                TheCourse++ )
            if( CourseID == m_Courses[TheCourse].GetID() )
                break;
        if( TheStudent == m_Students.size() ||
                TheCourse == m_Courses.size() )
            return( false );
        if( m_Enrollments.Register( m_Students[TheStudent],
            m_Courses[TheCourse] ) )
            return( true );
        else
            return( false );
    }
};
```

The Registrar class is the class that ties together all the other classes in our example. Although it is a simplified view of a registration process, it is functional for the purposes of our example. The Registrar class maintains an array of Student and Course objects as well as an Enrollments object, which in turn maintains a link between students and the courses in which they are enrolled.

It is possible for the Registrar class to have students who aren't enrolled in any classes, or courses without any students (just think, when a class is first added to the system, it starts out empty). The Registrar class is designed to mimic the registration process and to manage students. In this class, you will find the AddStudent, AddCourse, GetStudent, and GetCourse methods, which permit you to add and retrieve students and courses to and from the system.

Once students and courses are added, you can then begin registering students for courses. You can also add students, register them, then add other students and register them as well. However, our demonstration will not show this approach for the sake of simplicity.

The Registrar class also provides a Register method, which is used to register a specific student with a course. Diagramming the collaboration between classes is usually viewed as a small part of the entire application (described in more detail next), and an application may have many such diagrams. The sample diagrams we present later on apply specifically to the Register method of the Registrar class.

UML Sequence Diagrams

Ever see a map of the universe? Probably not a detailed one because a detailed map would simply be too large and complicated to represent with any level of detail on a single piece of paper. The way things really work is that a map has enough detail to get you to another smaller, more-detailed map. So, we can see using a map of the United States to locate New York, and then using a map of New York to locate New York City, and then a map of New York City to locate Central Park.

When we use diagrams to represent programs, the same logic holds true. It would be too complicated to represent an entire program with any level of detail in a single diagram. As we show diagrams here, you will have to remember that they represent a different scale or level of detail, typically broken into a specific feature of the application.

A UML (Unified Modeling Language) sequence diagram is a diagram that shows the typical sequence of events for a process. It is not a flow control diagram, which also contains conditional logic for branching, such as an if or while test.

Sequence diagrams are organized as a set of columns, where each column is an object and shows (using arrows) how each object interacts with the other. At the top of each column, a class name and optional object name (for use in the diagram) are used in the format Object: Class. Down the columns, arrows are used to represent a method called by one of the objects to identify the collaboration between the objects. If a method needs an object parameter, that's when we give one of the columns the optional object name.

The arrows in a sequence diagram are solid lines for method calls, and dashed lines for their optional return values. The columns or lines descending from the class names are called "life lines" and show the life span of the object.

Is main() a Class?

The UML sequence diagram is useful to represent how classes interact. This raises an interesting question with C++: Is main() a class? (The answer is, of course, no; it's a function.) The reason this question might be asked is, if the sequence diagram represents interactions between classes, then what interacts with that interaction?

In other words, if we have a diagram showing how to register a student, then what called the StudentRegister method that the diagram represents? That code is probably in a menu somewhere. Okay, so what interacted with that menu? Well, if the language is C++, there's a good chance it was main().

And therein lies the question: If main() is a method and not a class, how can we show the interaction of something that isn't a class using a sequence diagram? The answer is, we wouldn't. Ideally, the C++ program's main() method would actually just be invoked to create some sort of RegistrationApp class that is, in essence, the main application object. Using this, we can safely ignore main().

This doesn't come up as often in Java or C#, where everything must reside in a class.

Student Registration

Let's use our new classes and work on some nifty diagrams. We will start by defining the classes that represent the registration process: Student, Course, Registrar, and Enrollments, as shown in Figure 9-1.

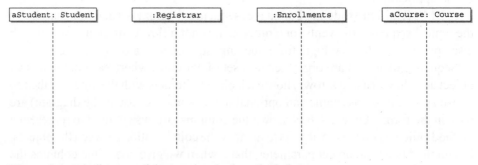

Figure 9-1   A diagram of the previously described classes

The process of registering for a course begins at the point where the registrar has already been asked to register a student (aStudent) for a course (aCourse). Here's what happens next:

- The registrar first checks whether the student is already registered by asking the Enrollments object to find a specific LinkCourseStudent using the Find function.
- The Enrollments object asks the aCourse object for its unique ID, which is returned as cID.
- The Enrollments object asks the aStudent object for its unique ID, which is returned as sID.
- The Enrollments object then does a search of its own LinkCourseStudent objects for one that has these two IDs (cID and sID).
- The Enrollments object then returns a Boolean value called isRegistered if the particular item is found.

We are only outlining one small section, which is to make sure that the student isn't already registered. The Registrar object would go on to interact further with the Enrollments object to make sure the class isn't full, then with the Student object to collect funds, and then with the Enrollments object again to add the student to the course. Figure 9-2 shows the completed sequence diagram for our registration process.

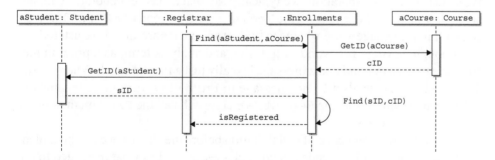

Figure 9-2 The completed sequence diagram of the registration process

UML Collaboration Diagrams

UML collaboration diagrams are used to display basic interaction with classes. Whereas the sequence diagram shows a detailed step-by-step collaboration between objects, the collaboration diagram is more a simplified, bird's-eye view of the collaboration.

Collaboration diagrams merely need to show the objects and their basic connections. You can optionally include the methods that actually perform the collaboration, and their sequence, by listing the methods next to the connecting lines with a number indicating their sequence. Of course, if you do this, what you would typically accomplish is a very complicated diagram that's best suited for the sequence diagram.

Figure 9-3 shows the collaboration diagram for our previous example. It shows that the Registrar class interacts with the Enrollments class, but not directly with the Course and Student classes. The Enrollments class, however, interacts with the Student and Course classes.

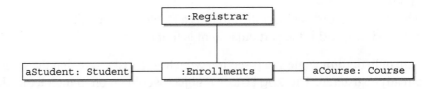

Figure 9-3   A UML collaboration diagram

Messages

When discussing collaboration, we typically say that a class collaborates with another via a *message*. For example, the Registrar class sends the Enrollments class a "Find" message to see whether a student and course are already registered.

Although *message* is a wonderful design and analysis term, as a programmer you have to keep in mind that a message is really just a function call. When we say that Registrar sends a Find message to Enrollments, more technically what we are saying is that the Registrar class will call the Find method in the Enrollments class.

By designing the sequence of collaboration before the classes, we can help identify what methods will be needed in what classes, as well as what they need to do, what they will accept as parameters, and what they will return as optional return values. For example, we now know that the Enrollments class needs a Find method.

The use of the term *message* to refer to a method call is really nothing new. In Windows programs, we often refer to Windows sending a "paint" message to a window so that it can redraw itself (if, for example, it was behind another window that was just closed). In Windows programming, applications have a `WndProc` (or window procedure) function, which the Windows operating system calls with the given message. The C prototype for this function looks like the following:

```
LRESULT WndProc( HWND hWnd, UINT Message,
        WPARAM wParam, LPARAM lParam );
```

The exact implementation of this function isn't important, but look closely at the second parameter: `Message`. When Windows wants an application to redraw itself, it finds the `WndProc` for the given main window (don't ask how Windows knows where it is, that's its job) and calls the `WndProc`, passing `WM_PAINT` as the second parameter.

This provides an interesting way of handling messages: Although we stated that a message is simply a function call, it is possible that several messages may be handled by the same function. As long as the information as to what message is being sent is passed to the method, it can handle any number of messages.

Collaboration and Inheritance

Collaboration in itself is not closely related to inheritance, but it can raise some interesting questions about design vs. coding. For example, we have an `Enrollments` class that we never saw before. That class is really nothing more than a collection class of some other type.

The `Enrollments` class might in fact be a *vector* class in C++, Java, or C# (except that we specifically use the `Find` method). So, if the `Enrollments` class is really one of these other classes, why not show that class name instead? Well, because `Vector` isn't quite as descriptive as `Enrollments`.

It's more likely that the `Enrollments` class is derived from the vector class, with some additional functionality added. The problem is, we have two people, or we wear two hats: the designer and the programmer.

The designer might say, "I want an `Enrollments` class," but the programmer might say "You already have one; it's called `Vector`." Although code reuse is always important, don't lose sight of your goal: to design, build, and deliver a working application.

You would most likely choose to have the `Enrollments` class derived from the vector class and provide the additional features as needed. You could opt to use the optional Object: Name in the sequence diagram, such as "`Enrollments: Vector`," but just the mention of the name "vector" might cause confusion on a design scale.

Association

Which came first, the chicken or the egg? We could ask the same question about association and collaboration. *Association* simply means that a class some how interacts with another class. Well, if they interact, then they collaborate. In order for there to be collaboration, there must be association.

This association means that the two classes need to know how to interact with one another. They need to know the other's methods, return values, and so on. We aren't breaking the encapsulation rules here, because the two classes don't need to have detailed knowledge of how the other works. They just need the basics, the interfaces.

This is normal methods and accessor methods come into play. Class design isn't just "need a class, design a class." Using our diagrams and understanding collaboration both contribute to the design of a class. As we see the class might need to collaborate with other classes, we add more functionality or interfaces.

If we clearly define the collaboration for all our classes, and therefore their association, we can create a clear definition of the class needed. With few exceptions (particularly in the area of testing and debugging methods), any methods not used in a diagram should not be added to a class.

It would by typical to start designing a class by thinking, "Okay, what does this class need?" However, that would probably be a mistake. You can't define the class on its own unless it's a very generic class such as a string or vector class. You have to know exactly how a class fits into the scheme of the application, and how it will be used, before you can start designing the class.

Avoid adding methods to classes "just in case." Wait for a need to arise and then add them. This need, of course, should arise during the design phase.

Self-Collaboration

Objects can collaborate with themselves as well as other objects. In our registration example, note how the sequence diagram shows a circular arrow that states "Find." This means that the Enrollments class calls its own Find method after getting the ID of both the student and course.

Although it is sometimes helpful to just point this out, it can also lead to the design of a given class. For example, we discussed in previous chapters that classes typically have private, public, and protected data members. Though not always the case, we might consider that self-collaboration methods are protected or private methods in a class, not accessible from the outside world.

Self-collaboration can occur as a single method or as multiple methods. Consider the following scenario: The Enrollments objects needs to save itself to disk. In order to do this, it would probably do something such as save the count of elements it has to disk and then save each element—something like the following pseudo code:

```
void Enrollments::Save( File )
{
   int I;
   WriteInt( File, GetCount() ); // Write count of elements
   for( i=0; I < GetCount(); i++ )
   {
      GetAt(i).Save( File );
   }
}
```

You can see that the `Save` method of the `Enrollments` class is calling its own `GetCount` and `GetAt` methods to save the data to disk. The `Enrollments` class's `Save` method calls the `Save` method for each of its elements. Note that to implement this functionality, our demonstration classes would all need to be modified to include `Save` and `Load` methods. To keep things simple, the preceding code is pseudo code and not actually implemented in the `Enrollments` class described or the sample source code for this book.

Class Responsibility Collaborator

As you saw in the "UML Sequence Diagram" section, sequence diagrams typically show a small part of the detailed interaction between two classes. A typical system would have many such diagrams, and the diagrams themselves might even be to different "scales" to describe certain degrees of abstraction.

The Class Responsibility Collaborator (CRC) diagram is intended to be an all-inclusive list of how a single class is to be designed. As you create and maintain your sequence diagrams, you will also want to maintain your CRC diagrams as well.

A CRC diagram lists the class name at the top and then two columns below for responsibilities and collaborators. It does not make an attempt to define the collaboration itself, such as what methods are called. Figure 9-4 shows a CRC diagram for our `Enrollments` class.

Enrollments	
LinkCourseStudent collection	Student
Find LinkCourseStudent	Course
Add LinkCourseStudent	
Delete LinkCourseStudent	

Figure 9-4   The CRC diagram for the `Enrollments` class

As you can see from Figure 9-4, the Enrollments class maintains a collection of LinkCourseStudent objects and provides methods to add, find, and delete these objects. It also interacts with the Course and Student classes.

The Enrollments class doesn't collaborate with the Registrar object because it doesn't call methods within the Registrar class. Although it is possible to define the collaboration with the Registrar class, the diagram could quickly become complex. At some point, we need to say that the collaboration stops at some level.

We also wouldn't diagram items in the CRC card that weren't directly collaborated with. For example, in Figure 9-2, the Student class doesn't directly interact with the Course class. Therefore, we wouldn't indicate this as a collaborator on the Student CRC.

NOTE: *CRC diagrams are often printed as a card and referred to as CRC cards. These cards can be helpful for the "brainstorming" process of the design.*

Quiz

1. What is collaboration?
2. What is a UML sequence diagram?
3. Are UML sequence diagrams usually all-inclusive diagrams?
4. Do UML sequence diagrams show flow control?
5. What does a dashed line indicate in a sequence diagram?
6. What does a solid line indicate in a sequence diagram between two objects?
7. What is a UML collaboration diagram?
8. Technically, what is a message?
9. Should you create diagrams using base class names if the derived object you are using doesn't use any methods outside its base class?
10. What is a Class Responsibility Collaborator diagram?

10

Case Modeling

So far, we have spent much of our time working on the design and creation of classes, and you've been given examples of how these classes can be created using diagrams and standard approaches. In this chapter, we are going to take a slight step back and talk about the overall design and analysis of a system, which in turn dictates the needs for such classes.

Although we will also be discussing classes and programming, it's important to point out that a fair amount of groundwork must be laid before the first line of code can actually be written. Even if you are not directly responsible for the design and analysis of a system, understanding and recognizing its workings will simply make you that much more valuable as a developer.

About Case Modeling

Consider the following architect paradigm: Architects are never told "Hey, make me a building." Instead, a tremendous amount of research and analysis goes into the process of designing a building that will meet the requirements of the buyer. In the creation of a software application, we need to adopt this same mindset.

You most likely won't be building an application that you will be using on a daily basis. You're building it for other people, the end users of the system. Although a good analyst can make useful recommendations to the buyer of the application, their first job is to identify the needs of the end user.

Another interesting comparison between architects and programmers is the detail of their design before starting the actual construction. I'm afraid that if most programmers were asked to create a building, they would build it, fill it with people, and then see if it fell down. Not a good approach. Architects, on the other hand, can tell you exactly how much weight any portion of any floor could withstand before it collapsed.

Of course, because an architect's creation holds people and is therefore responsible for human life, it demands a much higher degree of exactness than a program for which the end user can simply be told to "try again and see if the problem reoccurs."

Then again, a programmer might be creating an application for a heart monitor or Emergency Response System. And even if the programmer is just creating a game, the company's success and livelihood may depend on the success of this application. Therefore, you should examine your own programming tendencies and see if you can raise the bar for your professional attention to detail, no matter how experienced you are. Before you write the first line of code, you should have a clear, concise, and well-understood plan for the code you are about to create.

Oh No, Not End Users

Yes, end users. The jokes here can be endless in the technical community. The office assistant with the company for 30 years who still sees no reason why they just can't use a typewriter to write a letter, or when asked to send a copy of a disk sends you a Xeroxed copy.

Like it or not, these are the people who will be using your system. Never lose sight of the fact that you are developing a system for someone else to use—someone who may likely be using it on a daily basis, eight hours a day, for several years.

When designing a new system, you should work with the users. You are actually working for them. Take notes on all requests and desires, and don't think like a programmer yet. As a person is describing their needs about student registration, don't immediately start thinking "Okay, I can use a vector collection for that…." Take down all the information and the user needs, and think about the system. Even if you know you are going to be the person writing the code, design it as if you were creating the specification to hand off to someone else to actually code. In other words, be prepared to switch hats from designer to programmer, at a moment's notice.

Respect, patience, and attention to detail with all users will help ensure you a successful career. And, of course, you can also get some funny stories for your techie friends.

True story: While I was working in a service department in the early 1980s, a customer called with a problem. At the time, computers used 5.25-inch floppy disks, which had a small door on their drives that you had to close to hold the floppy in place. When I instructed the customer to place a diskette in the drive and close the door, they asked, "Why, is this confidential?"

Gathering Requirements

When designing a system, it is helpful to identify the people, organizations, or things that might interact with it. We call these things "actors" in the system. Note that an actor doesn't have to be a person. If a system needs to output a file in a certain format for a government agency, that agency might be considered an actor as well. Or, a board of directors may have influence over the rules of a system, in which case the entire board can be viewed as an actor. For the most part in our discussions here, however, actors will refer to people.

As you work with actors, you will certainly want to track information about them, such as their name, contact number, e-mail address, position, and so on. Position, however, does not necessarily play as vital a role as you might think in the design of a system. You might have two actors in developing a mail-routing system: the person who distributes the mail, and the president who will be paying for the system. In reality, the design of the system will be more driven by the person who actually distributes the mail than the person who pays for it. Of course, everyone gets to add their input.

Your first step is to identify who the actors in the system are and try to categorize them by their expertise of the system. For example, in our student-registration system, the registrar might be familiar with the typical daily operations of the office, but the Dean of Enrollments Management might have a more intimate knowledge of the policies that dictate enrollment or might even have knowledge of future changes.

We identify such actors as *subject matter experts*, or SMEs. These people, although they may not be using the system on a daily basis, have an expert knowledge of the system you are trying to automate.

You should start your interviewing with the SMEs. By doing this, you will gain a more intimate knowledge of the needs of the system and what the future needs might be for it. Also, you can identify which end users might also serve as good candidates for other interviews.

The Interview

It may seem obvious to state, but when you're performing an interview, be professional. Schedule the appointment well in advance, with several hours of time allotted. Arrive on time, and thank the person for their time in meeting with you. In your initial communication with the person, request that they have ready any sample reports or forms they currently use to do their job.

Have an agenda ready, and describe to the person the system you are going to create as well as how they fit into the system. Identify what benefits the system will have for them, and be sure to ask them what benefits they would like to see come out of it.

During the interview, ask the most important questions first, in case you run out of time. If a user begins to repeat something you have already heard, don't stop them by saying, "Yeah, I got that." Instead, use it as an opportunity to enforce your understanding and also to present the image that you are on top of things. Listen more than you talk, and take detailed notes on everything.

Make sure you follow up by summarizing your meeting in a nontechnical fashion, even if it's just a bulleted list, and send the person a copy of this document, thanking them again for their time.

It can also be beneficial to organize a meeting with several actors at once. Everything mentioned so far applies to a meeting with multiple actors as well, and you gain the advantage of not having to go back and forth between users to confirm "he said, she said." During a meeting, to some degree you will need to play the ringleader and encourage the discussion of ideas. First, listen to all ideas presented by members of the group and assess how the group responds to those ideas. Invite input from all in attendance to either accept, decline, or build upon the ideas. Encourage input from everyone.

Essential Use Case

An *essential use case* is a nontechnical view of how your system will work with its users. Its goal is to describe various aspects or operations, as well as who might perform these operations, be responsible for their input, or interested in their output. When you identify the actors of a system or create use case diagrams, you are performing essential use case modeling.

Figure 10-1 shows a simple use case diagram for our registration example. Note that it does not attempt to indicate a particular sequence or flow (such as a sequence diagram or flowchart would) but instead provides a graphic representation of the actors for our system along with their primary interaction with the system.

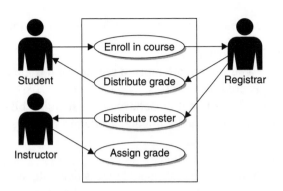

Figure 10-1   A simple use case diagram for the registration example

The people in Figure 10-1 are used to represent the actors themselves, and the large rectangle identifies our system. Inside the rectangle, text appears within ovals to identify particular tasks or needs for the actors. The arrows identify the initiation or start of the processes. Thus, we can deduce the following from our diagram (in no particular order):

- A student enrolls in a course.
- The registrar accepts the enrollment request and processes it.
- An instructor receives a roster.
- An instructor assigns grades for the course.
- The registrar distributes the grades for the course.

Note that we don't identify the details of the tasks. Does the registrar send an e-mail or regular mail to the student? If e-mail, is it sent via SMTP or an internal Lotus Notes mail system? What sort of database are the grades stored in? We can't tell from this diagram, and we shouldn't be able to.

The purpose of the use case diagram is simply to identify the use of the system, not its technical details.

Use case diagrams are accompanied by documentation that describes the actor(s) and the task(s) involved. At the very least, you should document the following items:

- The use case name
- A paragraph summarizing the diagram
- Prerequisites that must be met before a use case takes effect (for example, is the student eligible?)
- Results of the use case (for example, the student received her grade)
- The basic path that the use case takes (such as the numbered list just mentioned)
- References to business rules where applicable (described next)

An example of the documentation for an essential use case might be as follows:

- **Name**:   StudentRegister
- **Description**:   The student attempts to register, and if the registration is valid, he is registered for the class.
- **Prerequisites**:   The student must have no outstanding bills, not already be enrolled in the class, and be in good academic standing.
- **Path:**
    1. Student requests registration.
    2. Registrar approves registration and places data into system.
    3. System accepts or declines registration, and notifies registrar.
    4. Registrar notifies student of registration result via e-mail.
- **Results**:   The student is either registered in class or is not. The student is sent e-mail notification of the end result either way.

System Use Case

Whereas the essential use case approach defines the nontechnical aspect of a particular task or goal, the *system use case* defines the technical aspect. It is important to note that the use case diagram in Figure 10-1 can be used in both, as it demonstrates a particular task and its actors.

System use cases differ from essential use cases in their documentation and how we describe the process itself (as noted earlier, essential use cases are documented). Whereas the essential use case documentation would refer to the basic steps, needs, prerequisites, actors, and so on, the system use cases will document the technical aspects of the system, such as the user interface elements, database elements, and so on.

In describing a system use case, we might also find references to user interface elements, which are what make up the visual interface to the application. The most common user interface is Windows, and we can easily imagine using dialog boxes and controls (buttons, check boxes, list boxes, and so on) in the documentation process. Of course, not all programs or program steps require a user interface. Server-type applications don't have a specific user interface but can still benefit from system use cases to describe technically explicit operations.

Even the documentation here takes a bird's-eye-view of the process. We might describe our registration process in terms of "User login screen UI12 is displayed to retrieve the user's name and password" and "Logon table TBL3 is queried for a valid name and password combination." Note that UI12 and TBL3 are unique IDs given to a user interface element and a database table. As we design systems, we want a way to easily refer back to a specific item.

More technical (system) documentation for the use case diagram might look like the following:

- **Name**:   StudentRegister
- **Description**:   The student attempts to register, and if the registration is valid, she is registered for the class.
- **Prerequisites**:   The student must have no outstanding bills, not already be enrolled in the class, and be in good academic standing.
- **Path:**
  1. The student requests registration into a class using form UI12.
  2. The system checks business rules BR1, BR5, and BR9 to determine whether the student is eligible. If not, student is notified immediately.
  3. The system notifies the registrar of a new request using pop-up form UI11.
  4. The registrar reviews the data on form UI11 and approves or declines the registration.
  5. If the registration is approved, the system stores the registration data in Enrollments table TBL3 and sends an e-mail to student using the `Mailer` class.
- **Results**:   The student is either registered in class or is not. The student is sent e-mail notification of the end result either way.

Business Rules

No, we don't mean "business is the tops." It's a fact of life that we all have rules we must follow, and a business is no different. As you might guess, a business rule defines a rule a business must follow. For example, a business rule of our registration system might be that students can only enroll in a new course if they have paid for all their previous courses in full.

Any actor or SME of the system can define business rules. Going back to the "actor may be a government agency" example, a government agency might define certain rules under which a student is eligible for financial aid, and your system must implement those rules for each student.

Business rules are implemented in a method of a class. Let's go back to the "student must be paid in full" business rule for our registration example.

```
class Student {
   public:
      bool PaidInFull() {
         /* Search database to determine if paid in full */
      }
      bool Enroll( const Course& aCourse ) {
         if( PaidInFull() == false )
            return( false );
         else
         {
            /* Proceed with enrollment */
         }
      }
};
```

Note how the preceding class enforces the business rule about being fully paid. Because the business rule is placed in the `Enroll` method, it is now impossible to enroll students who aren't completely paid in full. Of course, there might always be waivers or special cases, so don't be surprised to find out there are exceptions to the rules. Hopefully though, if your actor interviews are done well, you can avoid these surprises.

We also decided to make the `PaidInFull` method a public method instead of a protected method (which would only be usable from within the `Student` class or one of its derivatives). We might decide that other portions of the system need to know whether the student is paid in full, without actually trying to do an enrollment to find out.

We might also create classes that are, in essence, nothing but business rules. There are times when COM and CORBA technologies work well with this, because these technologies are more "plug and play" adaptable than typical classes. In other words, if we have some sort of scheduling business rule class, and we identify that those business rules have changed, we can modify the one business rule class, which then can be used by a number of different programming languages or systems immediately.

COM stands for Component Object Model, and CORBA stand for Common Object Request and Brokering Architecture. Both provide a similar goal: to create a class that can be instantiated by different programming languages. For example, a COM class can be instantiated as an object by C++, Visual Basic, Java, and a number of other programming languages. COM is a Windows-based technology, whereas CORBA is found more on the Unix platform.

Business rules are documented in a numbered fashion, such as "BR1: Students must be paid in full before registration for any new classes will be accepted." These business rules are the outcome of your actor interviews and meetings, and often the SMEs provide the most detailed and accurate business rules.

User Interface Diagramming

The user interface is one of the more subjective aspects of programming. For the most part, we are talking about forms in which the user enters data, but the user interface is also composed of menu items and reports. Basically, whatever the user sees or interacts with defines the user interface.

Although programmers may tend to lay out the user interface in a manner they find both attractive and functional, the initial designs will often not be perfect the first time. As you design these sets of diagrams and forms, be prepared for change.

For example, we may think that the student's address comes before their grade information in the user interface. However, an SME might point out that the student's address is commonly entered just once, whereas the grade data is modified many times over the student's academic life. Having the address fields before the grades simply means the end user must move through those fields to get to the ones they work with the most, thus wasting time.

Use of screen real estate is also important. Try to fill up the screen with as much data as possible, but leave a consistent amount of space (both horizontal and vertical) between the controls on a form. If there is simply too much data to display on a single page, consider adding user interface elements specifically designed to handle this situation, such as tabs or pages, depending on the platform.

User Interface Flow Diagramming

User interface flow diagramming lets you define the flow of the program, from a menu selection to a specific form, then to another form or dialog box. As with all diagrams, the basic goal is to identify what is needed and how things should work. User interface flow diagrams are most often used to define how the user will interact with the system for a particular use case.

Figure 10-2 shows a simple user interface flow diagram for our registration example. The text on the lines between the boxes indicates the form or user interface element to be used at that particular stage, and the boxes contain the text defining the operation or stage. In this example, we can see the following:

- The student (user) selects the Register option from the main menu.
- The student is then presented with a form titled Enrollment.

- From the Enrollment form, the student must select a class. To enable them to do this, the Course Selector form is displayed.
- Once a course is selected, the student then selects a section (or schedule) for the desired course using the Selection Selector form.
- Once the student is registered, he is shown the Enrollment Verification form, which displays the summary of his new registration.

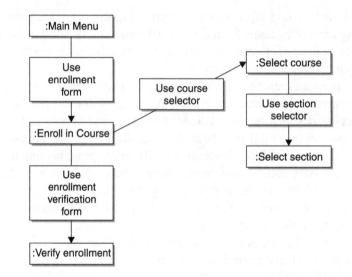

Figure 10-2   A simple flow diagram describing the user interface for the registration example

Note how we have each section or step of the user interface designed in terms of flow, including the course selection, section selection, and confirmation. Every aspect of the program must be accounted for.

User Interface Prototyping

User interface prototyping initially uses a diagram to define basically what will be displayed on a specific form. We can't write source code for a form until we know exactly what's on it.

Figure 10-3 shows a simple user interface prototype diagram. Note that at this stage, we don't care about the specific types of controls and their layout. We are still in the design and analysis phase, and spending too much time here in perfecting a user interface screen would be a waste of time because it is a commonly changed aspect of most programs.

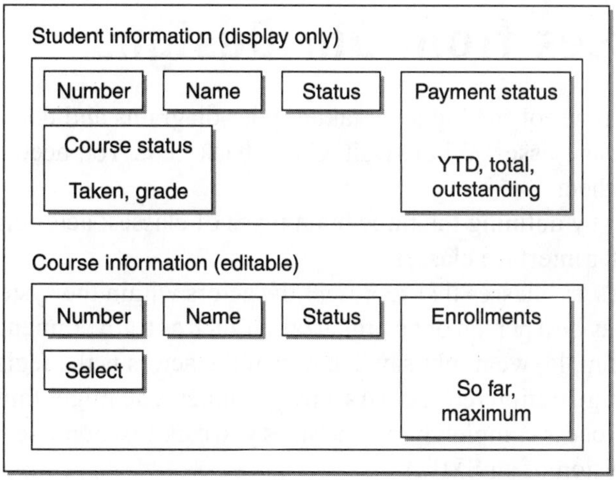

```
┌─────────────────────────────────────────────────────────┐
│  Student information (display only)                       │
│  ┌────────────────────────────────────────────────────┐  │
│  │ ┌────────┐ ┌──────┐ ┌────────┐  Payment status      │  │
│  │ │ Number │ │ Name │ │ Status │                      │  │
│  │ └────────┘ └──────┘ └────────┘                      │  │
│  │ ┌────────────────────┐           YTD, total,         │  │
│  │ │ Course status      │           outstanding         │  │
│  │ │ Taken, grade       │                               │  │
│  │ └────────────────────┘                               │  │
│  └────────────────────────────────────────────────────┘  │
│                                                           │
│  Course information (editable)                            │
│  ┌────────────────────────────────────────────────────┐  │
│  │ ┌────────┐ ┌──────┐ ┌────────┐  Enrollments         │  │
│  │ │ Number │ │ Name │ │ Status │                      │  │
│  │ └────────┘ └──────┘ └────────┘                      │  │
│  │ ┌────────┐                                           │  │
│  │ │ Select │                       So far,             │  │
│  │ └────────┘                       maximum             │  │
│  └────────────────────────────────────────────────────┘  │
└─────────────────────────────────────────────────────────┘
```

Figure 10-3   Boxes are used to group sets of one or more data elements.

Figure 10-3 uses boxes to group sets of one or more pieces of data. You can see that, at the top, the Student Information area shows the current student's ID number, name, status, payment status, and course status. We can imagine that Number, Name, and Status are all single fields. Payment Status, on the other hand, may have data such as how much the student has spent this year, in total, and how much they owe. This information is added at the bottom of the box.

Figure 10-3 also shows that, on the same screen, we have information about the course itself. It shows the number, name, status, and enrollments. It also provides a Select option, which could be a button that permits the user to pop up a list of all the courses offered by the institution.

As the user interface prototype is refined, you will eventually have defined all the components that need to be on a specific form. At this point, you may want to consider making actual prototype screens or mock programs. Doing this permits users to actually see, and possibly interact, with the real screens. A number of professional tools are available that permit you to create mock screens, but you may want to consider simply making them in the actual programming tool you will be using for the project.

The benefit to creating the mock screens using the actual programming tool is that you can then, if the design is approved, go ahead and use the code in the actual program. If you use a design tool (unless it specifically exports its design to your programming tool) to create a picture only, you will need to re-create the form from scratch in your development tool. Many Rapid Application Development (RAD) tools such as Visual Studio .NET, Delphi, and JBuilder make creating these mock screens very simple.

Defining Classes from Our Designs

Okay, now its time for the big step: taking your diagrams and documentation and start coding your classes. Whoa, wait. Come back here. You need to *design* them first, not code them.

We can start by defining the three main types of classes: actor classes, business classes, and user interface classes.

Actor classes are classes that represent the actors within the system. Remember that an actor may be a person or an organization such as a government agency. In our registration example, we might say that one of the actors is the registrar who must approve each registration request. (As a programmer, you might think that you can automate the process completely, and perhaps you can. Just don't be surprised if this becomes a decision of an SME.)

Business classes are the classes that define the business rules, or the main logic of the application. For example, we may have an Enrollment class that governs and enforces the rules for enrolling in a class. Business rules (as described earlier) can get quite complicated, and it is common to have multiple business classes in an application, some of which collaborate with others. Sometimes, business classes can be thought of as representing the actors within a system that are not soft-shelled creatures (in other words, *humans*), such as a government agency.

User interface classes are classes that implement a specific user interface feature. Examples of these might be the CFormView class in MFC, the JPanel in Java, and the Form class in C#. Of course, these are really just base classes in their respective languages, and we would design new classes derived from them to add the desired functionality and controls we need in our application.

In earlier chapters, we discussed the process of designing classes. Simple rules such as describing the requirements in plain English will yield nouns and verbs. The nouns become classes, and verbs become the methods of the classes. It would also be good to take into account the Class Responsibility Collaborator (CRC) diagrams and cards we discussed in the previous chapter, to help define the classes themselves.

We should also discuss something that typically does *not* become a class: possessive nouns. If something is a possessive noun, such as "student ID," then it most likely isn't a class but rather a property or attribute of a class. Of course, then again, it may be a class. We can easily identify that IDs come in various formats, such as Social Security numbers, ISBN numbers, and business tax IDs. For these, we may want to create a class to ensure proper formatting and validation when needed. The rule is, as always, use common sense and rethink the problem a couple times before finalizing your solution.

Identifying Technical Requirements

Now, this really has very little to do with programming, but we also need to identify the technical requirements of the system. Technical requirements define what is needed by the system as well as what the system needs to do or be able to do in order to successfully accomplish its job.

Technical requirements are usually dictated to you, and you simply document and enforce them. They normally don't affect any classes or designs.

Let's imagine that we have decided to document our technical requirements as a sort of numbered list, where each item is described and uniquely identified. We will number our items using the format SR1, meaning System Requirement 1. Therefore, we might come up with the following:

SR1 Host System
The system must be hosted on the university's existing Acme computer system. A browser interface and web connection is to be used for the user interface.

SR2 Database System
The database system must utilize, and be stored on, the university's existing SQL Server.

SR3 E-mail System
A new e-mail server must be installed for the purpose of e-mail notifications. A new machine is to be purchased, installed, and properly set up to serve as the e-mail server.

SR4 System Metrics
The system must be able to manage 5,000 students per year, and 1,000,000 students in total. It must be able to manage 500 course offerings, of up to five sections each. Also, 250 instructors per year must be tracked, with a total history of up to 1,000 instructors.

Note how each item has a simple number, a brief description of what it is we need to ensure, and then a more descriptive paragraph of the actual requirement. Although these items may not have an important impact on the design of classes, they still might have some impact. For example, we can see that up to 250 active instructors must be logged, so while designing the `Instructor` class we might decide that a single-byte value is all that's needed to identify a unique instructor (byte values range from 0 to 255). Of course, this specific example is somewhat overly detailed, and using a simple two-byte integer is more convenient and practical.

Change Cases

Another aspect of design, which doesn't really directly impact class design significantly, involves change cases. It's a fact of life that things change. People change (and change jobs), business rules change, and government agencies change. Therefore, your program will also change.

Change cases are documented much like technical requirements, using a simple numbered text approach. What you want to do is identify portions of your system that may be eligible for change some time in the future, and document them.

These change cases should include a single-line description of the anticipated change, a possibility indicator of the chance the change will be needed, and what sort of impact the change will have on your system. By describing these changes now, management has the ability to try and manage them.

The project manager may decide that a specific section of a design is complete but then suddenly get wind of a new change. Based on the impact and likelihood of the change, the project manager may authorize the design to be modified accordingly, or they may simply defer the change until it is a certain requirement.

Here's an example of the documentation for change cases (note that "CC" in the numbering system refers to "change case"):

- **CC1**:   A telephone response system needs to be implemented.
- **Impact**:   Moderate. The existing user interface classes that work with the console need to have telephony-compatible versions created. The business rules and actor classes have been separated from the user interface, so these classes need not be aware of the change.
- **Likelihood**:   Likely. The Vice Dean wants this implemented, but the Dean does not. The Dean will be retiring next year, however.

Project Management

We're afraid the days of considering building a model car project are over. Software development is a full-time job, and indeed many organizations have at least one individual who operates under the title "Project Manager" to help make sure that a project is completed successfully.

So far, we have talked about gathering requirements and the design and analysis phases, and the preceding section described change cases to handle program changes. We'll now discuss the final topic (which really isn't technically a programming issue): project management. We'll begin our discussion differently from any of the previous topics with the assumption that the designing, coding, and testing phases are already or nearly completed.

You can choose from a number of commercial packages to assist you in project management, such as Microsoft Project for general projects and StarBase StarTeam for software development projects. These applications basically help you to track and plan project progress.

We will take a hierarchical view of project management. Starting at the top, we will begin to drill down into the smaller details and identify some of the key aspects of each level.

Clients

This is a *really* a good place to start because the clients are the people who pay us. Keeping track of your clients is, of course, a primary goal. A client is usually a company, though some organizations develop software internally, in which case a client may be another department or cost center.

You should make sure you keep track of every contact at your client company, even if they leave. Keep their name, address, e-mail address, phone number, cell phone number, and so on. Make sure you have a good relationship with them, and know what they are responsible for. Identify who pays the bills, who approves the bills, who defines the business rules, who provides technical support, and so on. This sort of data is fairly common in all businesses, so it should be fairly straightforward.

It never hurts to provide a follow-up call on a project just to check the status and satisfaction of the client. Software development is a service-based business, and if your clients feel that you are providing a professional service, your success is all the more ensured.

Projects

Clients have one or more projects. All the design and analysis work we have done so far is organized into a project somewhere. A project is typically an application, system, or major change. An application is an individual program, whereas a system is a set of applications. A major change is an extensive amount of work needed to modify or change an existing application or system.

Projects should be documented with a brief description, a more detailed paragraph describing the system, the scheduled completion date, and the status and priority of the project. When we define the status of a project, we typically say it is either Initial Design, Pending Approval, Approved, In Progress, In Release, Completed, or Deferred. Priority is simply High, Medium, or Low.

Work Requests

Projects are made up of work requests, which define specific requests of the client. This is a very broad definition. A work request may be found at the very start of a project for the very first client meeting, or for a bug found in the system after it is placed into production.

Work is typically assigned one of the types shown in Table 10-1.

Type	Description
Work Request	A request to do some thing, such as create a backup, generate some statistics, or attend a meeting.
Defect	A defect is a bug report or a bug within the system.
Support	A request for assistance on a specific issue on the system.

Table 10-1 Work Assignment Types

Work requests typically have a brief description and a more detailed "Notes" section. The following items refer to the request, and a "Solution" section may also be present:

- **Project**   University Registration
- **Work Request**   Identify why reports are printing in landscape orientation
- **Type**   Support
- **Notes**   All reports printed in room 212 are printed in landscape.

A work request also has a priority (High, Medium, or Low) as well as a status and a responsibility. The Responsibility field identifies the person in your organization responsible for completing the work request. The status of a work request is typically one of the options shown in Table 10-2.

Systems can also determine whether a work request may generate other work requests. That is to say, someone may be assigned a work request of "Design registration system." That person then creates work requests for their employees, breaking this monolithic request into smaller requests, and so on. Managers use work requests in this manner.

Finally, a work request may be considered a milestone or significantly important somehow. The milestone may be the completion of a project or the end of a work request that indicates another pending request may now be started. Where applicable, you should document the milestones as well for the requests.

Status	Description
Pending Approval	The request must be approved before it's begun.
Approved	The request is approved and ready to begin.
Deferred	The request was deferred and may be reinstated later.
Closed	The request was closed and will not be reinstated later.
Duplicate	The request was a duplicate of another request.
Documented	Typically for bugs, this status indicates that the user misunderstood how the system operates, and they think a particular operation is problematic when in fact it isn't.
Completed	The request has been completed by your company.
Verified Completed	The client has agreed that the request is completed to their satisfaction.

Table 10-2   Status of a Work Request

Tasks

Tasks represent the lowest detail of work, and work requests are linked to them. Tasks are often used for the purposes of estimating and billing. As a programmer, you may receive a work request of "Create enrollment form." You would then enter one or more tasks to complete this work, with an estimate of the amount of time each will take you.

Once the tasks are begun, you would normally record the amount of time each task takes. Companies may have various rules of thumb on how these tasks are organized, such as stating that a single task should not take more than eight hours. So, what do you do if you estimate a task will take 40 hours? You break that single task down into smaller tasks.

Clients and end users normally don't see the tasks, as they are intended for the people who normally do the actual work (such as programmers) and their managers. They provide the estimates and hourly accounting needed to manage a project. Where possible, you should put in as much detail concerning your tasks as possible.

Tasks also have a priority and a status, with the status typically being one of the options in Table 10-3.

Status	Description
Open	The task is defined, but not yet begun.
In Progress	The task has begun.
Completed	The task is completed.

Table 10-3   Task Status

Estimation

Estimation can be an art form. No one but you can guess how long it will take you to perform a certain task. However, by knowing what needs to be done, breaking the estimates down into manageable tasks, and knowing your own abilities through your own experience, you'll find that estimation isn't very hard. Although an estimate is just that (an estimate, not a guarantee), you should make every effort to provide fair and accurate estimates.

The first step in the estimation process is to quantify. If asked to create a form, you have to know whether there are two edit boxes on that form or 20. For those edit boxes, you have to know which ones are stored in a table and which aren't. You also have to know which tables in a database are affected by the edit boxes, and so on.

Hopefully, these items are completely addressed in the design and analysis specification, like the user interface prototype described earlier.

You also have to know how to estimate each individual item. If the task is for something you are familiar with, this will be easy. If it's not a familiar task to you, however, this is where the real estimation process comes in. Based on your own talents, you have to guess how long it will take you to complete a task you may never have done before.

In these situations, you would do a small amount of research, try to gauge the task's difficulty, and compare this with your own expertise and ability to learn new things. Don't look at a new task and think, "Okay, two hours." Instead, do some research and try to be accurate. Then again, you don't want to suffer from "analysis paralysis," where you spend *all* your time thinking how you will perform the task.

Programmers have a tendency to fall into dangerous waters with estimates. Case in point: I had a specification for a program I knew had to be completed in two weeks. I gave that spec to a programmer and requested an estimate. About four hours later, the programmer returned with an estimate of exactly 80 hours, or two weeks. Although this was great news, I really had to question the programmer about the coincidence of the estimate matching exactly my deadline. Sure enough, the programmer's response was, "Well, you said you needed it in two weeks, so I'll do it in two weeks."

Such thinking makes a project manager's job a nightmare. Estimates aren't used just to see how long you think something will take, but rather to manage a project. If the programmer came back to me with a three-week estimate (which turned out to be the real case), I would know that I needed to add another programmer to the project. However, by trying to fudge his estimate to make me happy, he denied me the ability to make that decision.

Quiz

1. What is an actor?

2. What is a subject matter expert?

3. In your initial communication with a subject matter expert or an actor, what should you request from them?

4. What should be the first thing you do when interviewing a subject matter expert or actor?

5. What is an essential use case?

6. What is the purpose of a use case diagram?

7. What does the system use case define?

8. What is the purpose of business rules?

9. What do you use to define the flow of the program from a menu selection to a specific form?

10. What is an actor class?

11

Interfaces

The telephone is one of the many technologies we take for granted. You can go anywhere in the country and use a telephone to call home. You don't think twice about how to use the phone because, regardless of the manufacturer, all telephones have the same keypad and work the same way—they all have the same user interface. Anyone who learns how to use one phone can use the same skills to use any other phone. When you dial home, you are connected in a second, regardless of the technology used in the telephone. The concept of a common interface also applies to an object-oriented program, although not necessarily a user interface. In this chapter you'll explore interfaces used in object-oriented programming and how they increase the flexibility of program development.

Inside Interfaces

When a person in the computer industry hears the term *interface*, he usually thinks of a user interface, such as the Windows or Mac OS X operating system shells. Interfaces in programming serve a similar need, but at a very different level.

A user interface defines how a user interacts with a program. Thanks to modern graphical user interfaces (GUIs), users know how to exit or terminate the programs on their systems, even if it's the first time they've run a particular program. This standard approach of various programs on the same operating system leads to a reduced learning curve for new applications.

The interfaces we are interested in, however, are not user interfaces but rather interfaces for object-oriented programming and design. Simply put, an interface defines a set of methods needed to provide a particular feature or behavior in a class. An interface may also provide any number of attributes, but these are not required.

Because an interface defines a certain behavior or feature, we will be using it to add a behavior to a generic class. We can then write methods that take as a parameter the interface, but we can pass to that parameter the class that implements the interface.

Interfaces are supported syntactically by a number of languages, but we will be discussing only Java and C# here. C++ doesn't provide direct support for interfaces; however, there are some "tricks" we can perform to simulate their behavior.

Interfaces Are Not Classes

An interface might initially start to look like a class. Let's consider the previous definition a bit closer: "Simply put, an interface defines a set of methods needed to provide a particular feature or behavior in a class." Right about now you might be thinking, "Okay, so let's see here…something that defines a set of methods. Sounds like a class to me."

Ok, you got us there. Let's clarify a bit further: Although interfaces define methods, they do not contain any actual code. Fine, now you're thinking, "Are you wasting my time? I can create a class with methods, and make all the methods 'pure virtual' in C++ or 'abstract' in Java, and have the same thing." And a very astute observation on your part that is. Interfaces are very similar to classes that contain nothing but abstract methods.

But, consider this: Java and C# do not support multiple inheritance. This means that if you were to create two such classes with only abstract methods, you couldn't use both of them as your base class. And this is where, syntactically, interfaces are different.

Although Java and C# don't support multiple inheritance, they do support multiple interfaces. Therefore, if we wanted to define one interface to provide a behavior such as generating HTML output, and another interface to provide a behavior such as storing or retrieving itself to or from a database, we could do it.

Rather than create a class derived from another class with all abstract methods in it, we create a class that "implements" an interface. "Hmmm," you might be thinking, "if an interface is like a behavior or feature, then I guess something that implements the interface could be said to 'implement a behavior' or 'implement a feature.' Why, then, don't they call an interface a feature or a behavior?" Well, if they called it a behavior, someone would have said, "Gee, that sounds like an interface to me."

In summary, because an interface doesn't provide any code and requires you to write code in your class, this isn't "inheritance." Therefore, multiple interfaces don't qualify as multiple inheritance.

Interface Diagrams

You have two principle ways in which to diagram an interface: You can diagram the interface itself, and you can show within the diagram that a class implements the interface.

Figure 11-1 shows a diagram that represents an interface. The first line, called the *stereotype,* describes what the box represents, and the second line provides the name of the interface. Below that you find the methods of the interface. You can then optionally create a diagram that has an arrow going from a class to the interface, to indicate that it implements that interface.

Figure 11-1   A typical interface diagram

Figure 11-2 shows a diagram using a type of shorter notation, referred to as the *lollipop notation.* This notation doesn't provide details about the interface but rather merely that a class implements it. The interface name appears in the circle, and a line connects it to the class that implements it (in this case, `Course`).

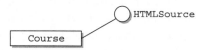

Figure 11-2   This diagram shows that a class implements the interface.

The shorter notation obviously saves space and is simpler to reproduce, but it's best used for well-known interfaces, whether in the language or the application itself.

Show Me the HTML

In order for you to understand interfaces, we'll start out with a conceptual example. We have been working with a school registration system throughout the book, so we'll stick with that example. In our registration system, so far we have seen similar (or derived) classes such as `Student` and `Instructor` (potentially derived from a `Person` class) as well as dissimilar classes such as `Enrollment` and `Course`.

Because `Course`, `Person`, and `Enrollment` are dissimilar, they probably won't share the same base class (we'll discuss "super" base classes later). But, as it turns out, we may want to have a standard method in each of these classes to permit us to display the data of an object.

Because we have already discussed a `Display` method common to each of the classes, let's make this example a bit more interesting. Our goal is to introduce a standard method, called `GetHTML`, for objects to generate their own HTML source for display in a web page.

Now you might be jumping ahead here. Perhaps you are thinking, "Why do I need this 'interface' thingy? Why can't I just add the `GetHTML` method to the desired classes?" Well, the fact is, we will be doing this, but you will see how interfaces permit us to treat classes such as `Student` and `Course` as generic providers of HTML data, rather than as two distinct classes.

A Quick Introduction to HTML

If you've been on the Internet, you have seen HTML in action. The Hypertext Markup Language defines the appearance and content of a web page. When you visit a website, typically your browser asks the web server for an HTML file, which the server "serves up" to you. Your browser then follows the HTML commands (or "tags") and renders the proper appearance intended by the author of the HTML file.

Although some web pages can be fairly complicated, you can normally visit any web page and view the HTML source for that page. In Internet Explorer, you would select View | Source from the main menu to view the HTML source for the current page.

HTML is defined as a set of tags that control the formatting of a page. These tags normally are used in pairs, where the text or content of the web page is wrapped by the tags. Table 11-1 gives a brief summary of the common HTML tags, some of which we will be using in our example:

Start tag	End tag	Description
 	None	Indicates a line break.
<B>	</B>	The text between the tags is displayed in a bold font. Example: <B>Bold</B> text.
<P>	</P>	Denotes a paragraph. Example: <P> Paragraph1</P><P>Paragraph2</P>
<TABLE>	</TABLE>	Denotes a tabular or columnar table.
<TR>	</TR>	Denotes a row within a table.
<TD>	</TD>	Denotes a cell or column within a table. Example: <TR><TD>Jones</TD><TD>Tom</TD></TR>

Table 11-1   Common HTML Tags

The HTMLSource Interface

We want to create our own interface, which we will call HTMLSource. The feature this interface will provide is the ability to format its data as HTML.

Now, before we go much further, you should be aware that providing user interface functionality in a class that also implements some sort of logic or rule functionality is typically considered bad design. Ideally, logical classes are separated from user interface classes. A more realistic example would be to provide an XMLSource interface to provide XML-formatted data. However, XML and its usage are more complicated than we have space to cover.

The HTMLSource interface we'll create will have a single method, GetHTML(), that returns the object's data in an HTML-formatted string.

The interface in Java would look like the following:

```
package Registration;
public interface HTMLSource
{
    public String GetHTML();
}
```

Note the use of the `interface` keyword to declare `HTMLSource` as an interface, not a class. Inside you can see fairly typical method signature:

```
public String GetHTML();
```

This means that `GetHTML` is a method that accepts no parameters and returns a string. Note, however, that unlike a normal Java class, the body of the function is not defined as or marked "abstract." By being in an interface, it is implicitly abstract.

The same interface in a C# program would look pretty similar:

```
namespace Registration
{
   public interface IHTMLSource
   {
      string GetHTML();
   }
}
```

Again, C# uses the same `interface` keyword, which is followed by the interface name, and inside you find the return data type, method name, and argument list but not the body of the method. Note that by popular convention (but not by requirement), interfaces in C# normally start with the letter *I*.

The Classes, Before an Interface Is Implemented

Our example will use four classes: `Person`, `Student`, `Instructor`, and `Course`. The class `Person` will provide the first and last name attributes (data members) and will serve as the base class for `Student` and `Instructor`. The `Course` class will not be derived from anything, and for the sake of simplicity will contain nothing but the course name.

The Java classes are defined as follows:

```
/////// Person.java
package Registration;
public class Person {
   protected String FirstName, LastName;
   public void Modify( String First, String Last )
   {
      FirstName = First;
      LastName = Last;
```

```
  }
  public void Display()
  {
    System.out.print( FirstName + " " + LastName);
  }
}


/////// Student.java
package Registration;
public class Student extends Person {
  protected int GraduationYear;
  public Student() {
    GraduationYear = 0;
  }
  public void Modify( String First, String Last, int Graduation ) {
    super.Modify( First, Last );
    GraduationYear = Graduation;
  }
  public void Display() {
    super.Display();
    System.out.print( " " + GraduationYear );
  }
}

/////// Instructor.java
package Registration;
public class Instructor extends Person {
  protected boolean IsTenured;
  public Instructor() {
    IsTenured = false;
  }
  public void Modify( String First, String Last, boolean Tenured ) {
    super.Modify( First, Last );
    IsTenured = Tenured;
  }
  public void Display() {
    super.Display();
    if( IsTenured )
      System.out.print( " (Tenured)" );
    else
      System.out.print( " (Not tenured)" );
  }
}
```

```java
/////// Course.java
package Registration;
public class Course {
  protected String Name;
  public Course() {
  }
  public void Modify( String CourseName ) {
    Name = CourseName;
  }
  public void Display() {
    System.out.print( Name );
  }
}
```

The matching classes in C# would be declared as follows:

```csharp
/////// Person.cs
using System;
namespace Registration
{
    public class Person {
        protected string FirstStr, LastStr;
        public void Modify( String First, String Last ) {
            FirstStr = First;
            LastStr = Last;
        }
        public void Display() {
            System.Console.Out.Write( FirstStr + " " + LastStr );
        }
    }
}
```

```csharp
/////// Student.cs
using System;
namespace Registration
{
    public class Student : Person
    {
        protected int GraduationYear;
        public Student() {
            GraduationYear = 0;
        }
        public void Modify( String First, String Last, int Graduation )
            {
            base.Modify( First, Last );
```

```
            GraduationYear = Graduation;
        }
        public void Display() {
            base.Display();
            System.Console.Out.Write( " " + GraduationYear  );
        }
    }
}

/////// Instructor.cs
using System;
namespace Registration
{
    public class Instructor: Person
    {
        protected bool TenuredBool;
        public Instructor() {
            TenuredBool = false;
        }
        public void Modify( String First, String Last, bool Tenured )
         {
            base.Modify( First, Last );
            TenuredBool = Tenured;
        }
        public void Display() {
            base.Display();
            if( TenuredBool )
                System.Console.Out.Write( " (Tenured)" );
            else
                System.Console.Out.Write( " (Not tenured)" );
        }
    }
}

/////// Course.cs
using System;
namespace Registration
{
    public class Course
    {
        protected string NameStr;
        public void Modify( String Name  ) {
            NameStr = Name;
        }
```

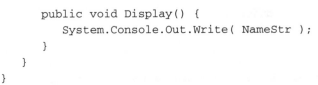

```
    public void Display() {
        System.Console.Out.Write( NameStr );
    }
  }
}
```

Implementing Interfaces in Java and C#

Now that our classes are defined, we need to actually implement them. We need to indicate in the class declaration that we intend to implement the interface, and we also need to write the methods that are contained in the interface.

In Java, we write the following to modify the Student class:

```
/////// Student.java
package Registration;
public class Student extends Person implements HTMLSource {
   protected int GraduationYear;
   public Student() {
      GraduationYear = 0;
   }
   public void Modify( String First, String Last, int Graduation )
   {
      super.Modify( First, Last );
      GraduationYear = Graduation;
   }
   public void Display()
   {
      super.Display();
      System.out.print( " " + GraduationYear );
   }
   public String GetHTML()
   {
      String Ret = new String();
      Ret = "<B>"+FirstName+" "+
      LastName+"</B> Graduates in "+
      GraduationYear;
      return( Ret );
   }
}
```

Note how the first line of Student has been modified to use the syntax implements HTMLSource, which means we will be implementing that behavior. The next step is to add the GetHTML method to the class (listed in the preceding code in bold font).

Taking the same approach for C#, we write the following:

```csharp
//////// Student.cs
using System;
namespace Registration
{
    public class Student : Person, IHTMLSource
    {
        protected int GraduationYear;
        public Student() {
            GraduationYear = 0;
        }
        public void Modify( String First, String Last, int
            Graduation ) {
            base.Modify( First, Last );
            GraduationYear = Graduation;
        }
        new public void Display() {
            base.Display();
            System.Console.Out.Write( " " + GraduationYear  );
        }
        public string GetHTML() {
            return "<B>" + FirstStr + " "+ LastStr +
                "</B> Graduates in " +
                GraduationYear;
        }
    }
}
```

In this C# example, note that the syntax for declaring that you are implementing an interface only requires you to list the interface name after the class name is declared. In the preceding code, we state that we are deriving from Person and are implementing IHTMLSource, because Person is a class and IHTMLSource is an interface.

Bringing It All Together

Having the classes functional and implementing the proper interface are important, but we are still missing the demonstrational code that shows why the interface is different from a class with only abstract methods in it. The answer is presented here, and it requires us to write a function that takes an interface (not a class) as a parameter.

In Java, we would write this as follows:

```
protected void ShowHTML( HTMLSource SomeObject )
{
    System.out.println( SomeObject.GetHTML() );
}
```

The C# version would be nearly identical:

```
protected void ShowHTML( IHTMLSource SomeObject )
{
    System.Console.Out.WriteLine( SomeObject.GetHTML() );
}
```

Now, in both Java and C#, we have a ShowHTML method that accepts any object that implements the HTMLSource interface. With this knowledge, it is safe for the preceding ShowHTML function to call the GetHTML method on the received object.

Figure 11-3 shows what our diagramming now looks like, with multiple classes that implement an interface.

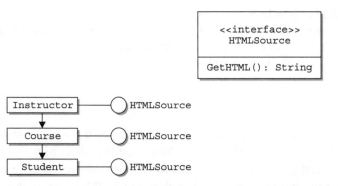

Figure 11-3   A diagram showing multiple classes that implement an interface

What About C++?

As stated at the beginning of this chapter, C++ does not provide syntactical support for interfaces. However, C++ does provide support for multiple inheritance. Earlier on we described how an interface is very similar to a class with all abstract methods. The problem in Java and C# is a lack of multiple inheritance, which means we can't use this type of class and therefore have to use interfaces.

In C++, thanks to multiple inheritance, we can do something very similar by using a class with all abstract (or pure-virtual) methods. Consider the following C++ class:

```
class HTMLSource
{
   public:
      virtual string GetHTML() const = 0;
};
```

Here we have a class with a single pure-virtual function, much like the Java and C# interfaces from earlier. Now, we declare a Student class, derived from the Person class *and* the HTMLSource class, and provide the GetHTML method:

```
class Student: public Person, HTMLSource
{
   public:
      string GetHTML()
      {
          return "<B>" + FirstStr + " "+ LastStr +
             "</B> Graduates in " + GraduationYear;
      }
      // Portions of class removed for readability
};
```

As in Java and C#, we write a function in C++ that takes an HTMLSource object as a parameter and can accept any class with HTMLSource somewhere in its ancestry:

```
void ShowHTML( const HTMLSource& Src )
{
   cout << Src.GetHTML();
}
```

Components

A component is a class designed to fit into some preexisting class framework. It may do so through inheritance or by implementing one or more interfaces, but it must follow the rules of components for the environment in which it is being developed.

The more common examples of components include the controls and beans found and used in modern Integrated Development Environments (IDEs). Java development tools and .NET Framework tools usually implement some type of form designer, where you can drag and drop controls such as buttons from a tool palette onto a form.

The items that appear in the tool palette are examples of the types of components we are talking about, and they are often written in the language of the IDE itself. For example, the `JButton` class in Java can be displayed in the tool palette of most modern Java IDEs because it was written to meet the requirements of doing so. You can drag the button from the tool palette, drop it on a form or panel, and then view the source code and see the declaration and initialization of the `JButton` object added to your source code automatically.

These types of components are a key aspect of Rapid Application Development (RAD) and have been popular for a number of years. The simplicity of the visual interface is very attractive for its speed and simplicity. You may even work with components visually at design time (while you build the application) even if they have no visual appearance at run time (while the program is executing).

An example might be an FTP component that provides File Transfer Protocol support but doesn't have a specific display at run time (too many things must be done to be wrapped up neatly in a user interface). In such a case, you still see a benefit to just dragging the component onto the form because this action is quicker and less prone to mistakes than manual typing. You can also normally use such components as normal classes (because they are, after all, classes) and manually declare and initialize them a needed.

Therefore, components typically implement the following types of behavior, using inheritance and/or interfaces specific to the language:

- **Support for introspection**   Allows an IDE to analyze how a component works.
- **Support for customization**   Allows a programmer to alter the appearance and behavior of a component.
- **Support for events**   Allows components to fire events and inform IDEs about the events they can fire.
- **Support for properties**   Allows components to be manipulated programmatically as well as to support any customization.
- **Support for persistence**   Allows components that have been customized in an application builder to have their state saved and restored. Typically persistence is used with an IDE's Save and Load menu commands to restore any work that has gone into constructing an application.

For Java, the component type is JavaBeans, whereas C# simply has "components."

Standard Interfaces

In order to help your understanding of interfaces, it's useful to take a look at what other developers have created. In this section we will look at some of the common interfaces provided by Java and C#. This is by no means a complete list of interfaces, but it will show you some patterns in how the architects of these languages and their associated class and interface libraries designed their systems.

As we discuss these interfaces, keep the following in mind: Interfaces implement a behavior, which implies some other code will be calling methods within the interface. In our example, although all our classes implement the `HTMLSource` interface, it's the `ShowHTML` method that makes use of the interface. You can consider interfaces as providing "callback" functions.

Standard Java Interfaces

The following is a list of some commonly used Java interfaces, with a brief description of each.

actionListener

The `actionListener` interface is implemented by classes that want to be notified of actions. This is commonly seen implemented in classes such as forms to respond to user interface events such as button clicks. The `actionPerformed` method is the only member of this interface.

BeanInfo

This interface is implemented by JavaBean classes that want to provide information about what they provide. See the section titled "Components" for more information on JavaBeans.

Cloneable

Classes that provide a valid clone method should implement this interface. It has no methods but is used to indicate whether it is safe to call the clone method for an object.

Collection

Classes that maintain a collection implement this interface. It has methods that work with collections such as `add`, `clear`, `isEmpty`, `size`, and so on.

Note that the predefined collection classes such as `LinkedList`, `Vector`, `HashSet`, and so on, all implement this interface.

Iterator

Classes that provide some sort of collection usually implement this interface. Methods in the `Iterator` interface include `hasNext`, `next`, and `remove`.

Serializable

Classes that have their data saved to and loaded from a stream implement this interface.

Standard C# Interfaces

The following is a list of some commonly used C# interfaces, with a brief description of each.

ICloneable

Implemented by classes that support the clone method.

IComponent

If a class is to be considered a component, it should implement this interface. Note that the `Component` class implements this interface.

IContainer

Classes that contain components implement this interface. For example, the `Form` class is derived from a class that implements this interface.

ICollection

Classes that maintain a collection of data implement `ICollection`. Many classes are precreated with this interface already implemented.

INumerator

Classes that provide iteration or enumeration implement this interface.

ISerializable

Classes that have their data saved to and loaded from a stream implement this interface.

As you can tell from these lists, interfaces tend to be generic behaviors, such as "implement a collection." You'll also note that Java and C# have similar interfaces. Interfaces make up a key part of how the JavaBeans and C# components work, in that they have predefined behaviors your new classes must implement before these classes can be considered a bean or component.

Ultimate Base Classes

Where do I begin? Many object-oriented programming languages (OOPLs) define a default class that all new classes are derived from, unless you specifically indicate a different base. Of course, if you do specify a different base class, your base class must have a base.

Java and C# both implement this "default ultimate class" behavior (C++ does not). In Java, if you don't specify a base class to a new class, it will default to the Object class as its base (or super) class. C# uses the same name, Object, for its ultimate base class.

Ultimate base classes are used for a number of reasons, but they are typically designed to permit you to work with data in a generic manner. When the designers of the Java and C# languages created their library frameworks, they implemented a design that would be extremely helpful most of the time, but sometimes would just not be applicable. To dive into this statement a bit further, let's look at the Java and C# ultimate base classes, listed in Tables 11-2 and 11-3, respectively.

Method	Access	Description
Object Constructor	Public	Initializes an object.
clone	Protected	Creates and returns a copy of this object.
equals	Public	Indicates whether some other object is "equal to" this one.
finalize	Protected	Called by the garbage collector on an object when it determines there are no more references to the object.
getClass	Public	Returns the runtime class of the object.
hashCode	Public	Returns a hash code value for the object.
notify	Public	Wakes up a single thread that is waiting on this object's monitor.
notifyAll	Public	Wakes up all threads that are waiting on this object's monitor.
toString	Public	Returns a string representation of the object.
Wait	Public	Overloaded versions. Causes the current thread to wait for some event or operation for this object.

Table 11-2   The Java.lang.Object Class

Method	Access	Description
Object	Public	This constructor initializes a new instance of the Object class.
Equals	Public	Determines whether two Object instances are equal.
GetHashCode	Public	Serves as a hash function for a particular type, suitable for use in hashing algorithms and data structures such as a hash table.
GetType	Public	Gets the type of the current instance.
ReferenceEquals	Public	Determines whether the specified Object instances are the same instance.
ToString	Public	Returns a string that represents the current object.
Finalize	Protected	Allows an object to attempt to free resources and perform other cleanup operations before it is reclaimed by garbage collection. In C#, finalizers are expressed using destructor syntax.
MemberwiseClone	Protected	Creates a shallow copy of the current object.

Table 11-3   The C# System.Object Class

With the exception of the threading functions in the Java class, you can begin to see some similarities in the design of the classes:

- They have a method to compare to objects.
- They have a method to clone a new object from an existing object.
- They have a method to convert an object to a string.
- They have a finalize method to destruct the object.

This certainly goes a long way toward polymorphism. Just image, any object in Java or C# has the ability to format itself into a string or to see whether it is equal to some other object. However, don't forget that someone, somewhere had to write that code. If you create a new class in Java or C# and you want that object to be able to convert a formatted string for itself implicitly, you would want to create a toString method in Java or a ToString method in C#.

So what's the downside to these ultimate base classes? For one, having all objects implement a toString method may simply not be practical. For example, if we had a class for creating and manipulating images, what would toString return for that? For this reason, these ultimate base classes are kept to a bare minimum.

How do these ultimate base classes tie into interfaces? As you'll remember from our discussion at the beginning of this chapter, we explored the similarities between an interface and a base class. We determined that although they are mostly similar, there are a few distinguishing differences. We could have, in theory, designed our examples for this class so that we have an ultimate base class of `HTMLSource` that provides an abstract `GetHTML` method and then provide it in each of our derived classes. However, we didn't do this for the following two reasons:

- First of all, we simply can't. The ultimate base classes for Java and C# are already defined, and we can't add a `GetHTML` method to them. The issue is that we can't go and change base classes (or we probably shouldn't, even if we could).
- We want to keep ultimate base classes simple and not add methods that are specific to a task or operation, such as dealing with HTML.

Quiz

1. What is an interface?
2. What is an interface diagram?
3. Why is an interface used in a program?
4. What is the difference between an interface and a user interface?
5. Does the C programming language use interfaces?
6. What kind of inheritance is similar to an interface?
7. Can an interface be used with C++?
8. Why do Java and C# support interfaces?
9. What is a component?
10. Give an example of a component.

CHAPTER

12

Object-Oriented Programming Languages

In this chapter we will dive into a discussion and comparison of several common and current object-oriented programming languages (OOPLs). But before doing that, however, we should really dive into a brief history of programming in general.

The primary difference between an OOPL and a purely procedural (non-object-oriented) language is that an OOPL provides a syntax to incorporate object-oriented concepts such as inheritance, polymorphism, and so on. Although the languages provide this ability on a syntax level, its important to recognize that OOP was not just "created," but grew out of good ideas and common practices of programmers.

A History of Computers and Programming

There really is no exactly defined start of computers—they can be traced to a number of origins, not the least of which is simply the creation of numbers and math itself. As you may be aware, all computers work internally with the binary numbering system, where all data is represented with 1s and 0s (because, being electronic devices, they have a state of on or off).

It may surprise you to learn that we will start our history discussion in the early 1940s. But to be more accurate, the groundwork was laid long before that. For example, the Fibonacci Series commonly used in programming exercises and used to define timing of recursive function calls was actually defined by the Italian mathematician Fibonacci in the thirteenth century!

In order to detail computer history, we first must define what a computer is. It can be argued that the abacus was a form of computer, but we will say that in order to be considered a direct ancestor of the modern computer, a computer must be able to store internally and execute a program. Amazingly, our history then starts in 1943, or several years before that if we take into consideration the designing stage of building a computer.

With the preceding definition, we would say that the first recognized digital computer was ENIAC (Electronic Numerical Integrator And Computer). ENIAC was built between 1943 and 1946 by the University of Pennsylvania for the United States government. It was designed to calculate bombing tables and trajectories for the military.

ENIAC was a behemoth of a machine, weighing over 30 tons, and containing more than 19,000 vacuum tubes (the predecessor to the transistor, "tubes" are electronic devices enclosed in glass, which you can still see today in many modern televisions) and 1,500 relays. In order to program the ENIAC, the technicians of the day would actually rewire the computer system, if a programming change was made. Truly a "hard-wired" system.

Around 1945, John von Neumann wrote a paper in which he outlined a method for storing a "program" in a manner more convenient to change. The ENIAC was modified so that it used switches to create a program. Instead of changing wires, programmers would flip switches to define the desired behavior.

In 1945, Grace Hopper became the first programmer to coin the term *bug*. One of her programs was not operating as expected. After checking her logic, she reportedly opened the computer system and found a moth stuck between two tubes. Amazingly, 60 years later, and the term *bug* is still used. Hopper also did a large amount of work on developing languages and compilers, and her work led to the creation of the COBOL programming language.

In 1946, Konrad Zuse developed the first high-level language, called Plankalkul. Although it was modeled on von Neumann's work, it contained a number of improvements over von Neumann's programming model. Zuse's work is not widely recognized in the computer industry, but he is sometimes attributed with building the first truly digital computer system.

In 1948, IBM created the Selective Sequence Electronic Calculator machine. Measuring 25×40 feet, this system used punch cards and tape to be programmed. In 1949, Maurice Wilkes built the EDSAC system, commonly thought of as the first stored-program system, which contained 1K words of memory. Wilkes had a set of punch cards he kept in a library for reusable procedures.

In 1950, Engineering Research Associates built the first commercially available computer: the ERA 1101. The first machine was purchased by the United States Navy and contained one million bits of memory on a magnetic drum. The year 1950 also saw the SEAC (Standards Eastern Automatic Computer) built by the National Bureau of Standards, which was the first computer to replace tubes with diodes.

The year 1951 saw the creation of the UNIVAC system by Remington Rand (who employed Grace Hopper at one time). This was the first computer to gain public attention and was the inspiration for a number of clones to come later, such as the MANIAC, ILLIAC, and SILLIAC.

Between 1949 and 1956, a number of small languages appeared. Languages such as A-0, Short Code, and AUTOCODE were designed to make the tedious task of assembling code easier. By modern definitions, *assembly language* is the language used by a particular CPU itself that these languages were all very close to. But, up to this point, there was no "central" processing unit, and what we now call a CPU was built from several distinctly different pieces.

In 1957, the first "modern" programming language made its appearance: FORTRAN (FORmula TRANslating), which is still in use today. In 1959, COBOL and LISP appeared, and in 1960, ALGOL 60, a predecessor for PASCAL, appeared. A number of languages and versions of languages began to appear during this time.

Between 1962 and 1967, SIMULA, the first object-oriented programming language, appeared. Simula II followed it in 1967.

In 1970, Kenneth Thompson, who created the UNIX operating system, created the B language so that UNIX would have a programming language for creating applications. The core of UNIX was originally created in assembly language, with various programs later developed in B. In 1972, Dennis Ritchie created the C language, based on the B language, which Thompson then used to rewrite UNIX. Also, 1973 saw the first published C reference book.

The year 1972 saw the introduction of Smalltalk, based in part on SIMULA. Smalltalk would be one of the more prevalent programming languages until C++ would appear.

Between 1983 and 1985, Bjarne Stroustrup created the C++ language, modeled after C. Originally called "C with Classes," this language would acquire ANSI standardization in 1989. C++ would be one of the major programming languages of all time, still in widespread use today.

In 1991, James Gosling, Patrick Naughton, and Mike Sheridan of Sun created Java. Java was originally intended to be a system for programming small devices such as cable boxes, and the programming language was only a small part of the system. Around 1995, the popularity of the Internet changed the intentions of Java, and Sun targeted it to be a multiplatform programming environment and language.

In 2000, Microsoft created the C# programming language, which was EMCA certified that same year. Often compared to Java, C# incorporates the same "environment" approach as Java, but it's currently still available only on the Windows platform (an open-source project is underway to create an open-source version of the .NET Framework for the C# language and the Common Language Runtime).

The Three Dominant Modern OOPLs

Certainly, we need to pay more detailed attention to the common object-oriented programming languages of our day. These are C++, Java, and C#, listed in order of their creation.

C++

C++ was created between 1983 and 1985 by Bjarne Stroustrup of Bell Labs. It was approved as an ANSI standard programming language in 1989 and has enjoyed widespread usage since the mid 80s.

Reusable Code

C++ has an extensive amount of low-level code prewritten in its standard library, but it mostly is geared toward collections and low-level data structures such as stacks and queues. Common programming tasks, such as working with databases, images, and Internet connections, are not provided by the C++ language itself but rather by add-on libraries or the operating system.

Performance

C++ is based on C, which is known as a high-performance language. Because of the many similarities, you will often see the two mentioned together, such as referring to a C/C++ topic, as we will be doing here.

C/C++ gains its high-performance advantage at the cost of ease of use. Although C/C++ lets you directly manipulate memory within the level of security provided by the operating system, doing so incorrectly is a common problem. C/C++ lets programmers directly work with any portion of memory they want, and it often requires programmers to manage their own resources. As you'll see, this fact leads to one of the most common misunderstandings about the C++ language.

Most programmers learn C before C++. Because C++ is based on C, this is a well-regarded approach. A typical topic in both C and C++ is pointers, which permit programmers to control dynamically allocated memory, work directly with any area of memory, and other tasks. When going from C to C++, most students continue to apply the C paradigm to this topic rather than the C++ approach.

For example, consider the following example in C, which is a function that loads a file into memory:

```c
char* Load( const char* Filename )
{
    char * pRet;
    FILE * File;
    int Size;
    File = fopen( Filename, "r" );
    if( File == NULL )
        return( NULL ); // Can't open file error
    fseek( File, 0, SEEK_END );
    Size = ftell( File ) + 1;
    fseek( File, 0, SEEK_BEG );
    pRet = malloc( Size * sizeof(char) );
    if( pRet == NULL )
    {
        fclose( File );
        return( NULL ); // Out of memory error
    }
    if( fread( pRet, sizeof(char), Size, File ) != Size )
    {
        fclose( File );
        free( pRet );
```

```
            return( NULL ); // File read error
    }
    fclose( File );
    return( pRet );
}
```

The Load function works properly, but look at the code and how it returns a pointer that it doesn't free. This is by design, and whoever calls this function must remember to free the memory. The misunderstanding is that many new C++ programmers still continue to write code like this. Instead, they should adapt the C++ approach by wrapping the code up into a class. Here's an example:

```
class TextFile
{
    protected:
        char* m_pText;
    public:
        TextFile() // Constructor
        {
            m_pText = NULL;
        }
        ~TextFile() // Destructor
        {
            free( m_pText );
        }
        const char* GetText() // Accessor function
        {
            return( m_pText );
        }
        bool Load( const char* Filename )
        {
            char * pTmp;
            FILE * File;
            int Size;
            File = fopen( Filename, "r" );
            if( File == NULL )
                return( false ); // Can't open file error
            fseek( File, 0, SEEK_END );
            Size = ftell( File ) + 1;
            fseek( File, 0, SEEK_BEG );
            pTmp = malloc( Size * sizeof(char) );
            if( pTmp == NULL )
            {
                fclose( File );
```

```
            return( false ); // Out of memory error
        }
        if( fread( pTmp, sizeof(char), Size, File ) != Size )
        {
            fclose( File );
            free( pTmp );
            return( false ); // File read error
        }
        free( m_pText );
        fclose( File );
        return( true );
    }
};
```

Note that in this example we could have used C++ streams to do the file operation, but we wanted to keep the code looking as similar as possible to the C example. The real demonstration here is that now the user of this class needn't be worried about releasing the memory allocated by the Load function.

Of course, "not worrying" isn't completely true. There are always exceptions to the rules, where common sense is the only true rule. What we think we have is a completely safe class that wraps and protects the m_pText pointer. Look, we even have an accessor function called GetText. But, consider the following problematic sample usage:

```
TextFile F;
F.Load( Datafile );
free( F.GetText() );
```

Note that here we are accidentally (and incorrectly) freeing the return value of the GetText, which is the m_pText data member.

Therefore, in this case C++ doesn't make it impossible to shoot yourself in the foot, only harder.

Performance: Compiled Code

C++ is a compiled language. This means that when you write the source code, you must compile and link it to get an executable. This executable is now in machine code for the specific computer on which it was compiled (although cross-compilers permit you to compile programs for other computers, such as building a Palm handheld program on a Windows PC).

Compiled code has a performance benefit over its counterpart, interpreted code. Compiled code, however, must be recompiled to be executed on another platform.

Security

C++ does not provide any sort of security. Any C++ program has the ability to access any block of memory or any resource it wants to (although operating systems such as Windows and UNIX have security to try and stop rogue programs from doing anything inappropriate).

Portability

Because it is an ANSI standard, C++ is the same language on all platforms. However, because C++ is a compiled language, you must compile an application before using it on a new platform. Because the user interface varies among platforms, this is one of the major issues in porting a program from one operating system to another.

Garbage Collection

C++ does not support garbage collection, the ability of a language to automatically clean up resources (memory, specifically) itself. In C++, if you allocate a block of memory, you are responsible for freeing it as well. The benefit to this feature is that destructors in C++ are true destructors. The downside is that it's possible through a programming error that a destructor is not called at all (which can result in resource leaks).

User Interface

The C++ language does not provide any user interface elements other than buffer console input and output. This means that it has no native support for graphical user interfaces such as Windows, Mac OS X, and the XWindow system. Instead, all these environments have their own application programming interface (API) that permits C++ to be used with them.

Multiple Inheritance

C++ provides support for multiple inheritance, which means that one class can have several simultaneous base classes (as opposed to multiple parents).

Templates

C++ provides a feature called *templates*. A template can be thought of as the mother of all macros. Templates are used like cookie cutters to define classes and functions that are used to create new classes and functions.

Templates are created using the `template` keyword and a format, which permits you to define parameters in the creation of the class or function. These parameters are more like empty holes in the definition that are filled when you actually create or use one of the objects or methods.

Here's an example of a template class definition:

```
template< class RealType >
class DataFile
{
   protected:
      RealType* m_pData;
      int m_Size;
   public:
      RealType GetAt( int Index )
      {
         if( Index < 0 || Index > m_Size )
            throw "Bad index";
         return( m_pData[ Index ] );
      }
      DataFile()
      {
         m_Size = 0;
         m_pData = 0;
      }
      ~DataFile()
      {
         free( m_pData );
      }
      bool Load( const char* Filename )
      {
         RealType * pTmp;
         FILE * File;
         File = fopen( Filename, "rb" );
         if( File == NULL )
            return( false ); // Can't open file error
         fseek( File, 0, SEEK_END );
         m_Size = ftell( File )  / sizeof(RealType);
         fseek( File, 0, SEEK_SET );
         pTmp = (RealType*)malloc( m_Size * sizeof(RealType) );
         if( pTmp == NULL )
         {
            fclose( File );
            return( false ); // Out of memory error
         }
```

```
        if( m_Size != (int)fread( pTmp, sizeof(RealType),
          m_Size, File ) )
        {
           fclose( File );
           free( pTmp );
           return( false ); // File read error
        }
        free( m_pData );
        m_pData = pTmp;
        fclose( File );
        return( true );
   }
};
```

In this example, the first line contains the `template` keyword, which contains one parameter: `RealType`. When we use the `template` class, we must define the value to be used wherever `RealType` appears within the template.

We declare a template object as follows:

```
DataFile<char> chFile;
```

Note that the class name is still `DataFile`, but we include the < and > brackets to define `char` as the value for `RealType`. Therefore, when the compiler sees this, it creates a brand-new class from `DataFile` and `char` (unless it has already created it). This is different if a class already exists, in which case you create an instance of the class. A template tells Java to create a new class unless the class already exists. This process means that the following code fragment from the original `DataFile` would go from

```
template< class RealType >
class DataFile
{
   protected:
      RealType* m_pData;
      int m_Size;
```

to this:

```
class DataFile
{
   protected:
      char* m_pData;
      int m_Size;
      class Person : public IDObject, public Instructor
      {
};
```

Java

Java was initially started in 1991 by James Gosling and others, with the intent of creating a smart environment for devices such as cable boxes. In 1995, however, its direction was changed to work with computers of all sizes. This change was due to the popularity of the Internet, and the diversity of the machines on which it ran.

Initially, Java adopted a "write once, run anywhere" approach, with the hopes of creating an environment that would enable programmers to create a program once and then run it on any type of device. In order to do this, the Java system was designed on several key components: the Java language, the Java Virtual Machine (JVM), and the Java API.

The Java language is, of course, the language itself and its given syntax. The Java Virtual Machine is a program running on a computer that interprets the "tokenized" source code of a Java program and executes it. Java is an interpreted, not compiled, language. The Java API is a rich set of classes that provides support for a wide range of features and capabilities in an application.

Java ran into two main problems, however: First, the initial Java Virtual Machines were not completely compatible between the various platforms. Typically, large applications would have parts of a program that would work okay on one platform, but not another, and vice versa. These initial incompatibilities meant that larger, robust systems would not be as reliable and functional as if a traditional programming language had been used.

The second issue Java ran into was that the "write once, run anywhere" philosophy was blown out of proportion. In reality, you can't create a typical desktop application and then expect it to work on a handheld phone computer because of the physical aspects: Desktops have much more memory, storage, and screen real estate than a typical mobile phone does. Although lower classes could be created for immediate use, designing systems for servers, desktops, and devices proved to be a tremendously different task and approach. To address this, Sun eventually released three different versions of Java, as listed in Table 12-1.

Edition	Geared Toward
J2EE Enterprise	Server or "enterprise" computing
J2SE Standard	Desktop PCs
J2ME Micro	Devices such as handheld PDAs and phones

Table 12-1   Editions of Java

Reusable Code

Java has an extensive collection of reusable classes. Common programming tasks such as working with databases, images, and Internet connections are built into Java, as are controls and user interface elements such as buttons and check boxes.

Performance: Interpreted Code

Because Java is interpreted, its performance is typically slower than that of a compiled language such as C++. The Java Virtual Machine interprets the tokenized "bytecode" of a Java program and executes it. The Java Virtual Machine is, in essence, a program that runs a program.

The benefit of the JVM however, is that the same tokenized code can run on different platforms without having to be recompiled, as long as that platform has a JVM.

Security

Java introduced a security model that stops programs from doing explicitly bad or dangerous things. Because programs run under the JVM, they can only do what the JVM permits them to do. Because the JVM does not permit a program to directly access memory, a Java program cannot do so.

The security model used by Java programs falls into two main categories: applets and applications. Applets are small Java programs specifically designed to be hosted in a web browser such as Internet Explorer or Netscape Navigator. Applets have a very strict security model and are prohibited from performing tasks such as creating connections to systems other than from the system that originated the web page. An applet can connect only to systems that generated the web page that contains the applet.

Applications implement security on a "sandbox" principle. This means that on a given computer, you can configure the various security attributes for an application and what sort of operations it can perform.

Because of its bytecode nature, however, security in Java is more open than in C++ in one particular aspect: Java programs are easier to decompile (the process of going from tokenized code back to source code). Although the source code generated by popular decompilation programs is hard to read, to say the least, it is much less complicated to read than a program that generates a compiled application (such as a C++ program). For companies wishing to protect their software from hacking or copyright infringement, this is not welcome news.

Portability

Portability has been one of the major strengths of Java. The ability to run the same program on a Macintosh as on a Windows PC makes it very attractive. The initial compatibility problems have been worked out (for some time), and this remains a very positive and robust feature of the language.

In order to run a program on a different operating system, you merely need the appropriate JVM installed on the computer. The problem is that there are several versions (not to be confused with "editions") of Java (version 1.5 will probably be released by the time you read this). A Java 1.4 program will not work on a computer that only has Java 1.2 installed. Many companies that distribute Java applications will install their own Java Runtime Environment (or JRE) to ensure the program will operate correctly.

As described earlier in Table 12-1, Java is available for servers, desktops, and handheld devices.

One of the disadvantages of Java is that there is no recognized standard. Whereas C++ and C# both have achieved some sort of recognized standard by a noncommercial committee, Java has not. Sun remains the owner and director of Java, and they decide how and when to change it. Sun recognizes that making drastic changes at this point in time would be a serious error, but the change from 1.0 to 1.1 was a major change that left many programmers wary of future changes. Furthermore, many companies such as HP and IBM are also greatly interested in furthering Java, and they have made their own non-Sun-approved additions (the SWT found in the open-source Eclipse project is a notable item).

Garbage Collection

Java implements garbage collection, meaning that you don't have to worry about releasing the memory you have allocated. If you create an object in Java, you are given a reference to it. If that reference goes out of scope, Java will automatically release any memory that the object used.

Consider the following C++ and Java examples:

```
// C++:
void Foo()
{
    DataFile* pFile = new DataFile;
    pFile->Open( "log.dat" );
}
```

```
// Java
public void Foo()
{
    DataFile File = new DataFile
    File.Open( "log.dat" );
}
```

In the C++ function, a `DataFile` object is dynamically created, and the `new` operator returns a pointer. We then use the `pFile` pointer to open a file and then just leave the function. Because C++ doesn't do garbage collection, the object allocated in `Foo` (and all the data it may contain) is lost because we don't do anything else with the pointer and we don't explicitly *delete* the object. The C++ `Foo` function, therefore, has a memory leak.

In the Java function, we are doing something similar. A new `DataFile` object is dynamically created, but we now get a reference to the actual object. As in the C++ example, we open a file and then leave the function. In Java, however, the JVM will see that the `File` variable (the only reference to the actual object) has gone out of scope and is no longer available. When the last reference to an object goes out of scope, the JVM marks the object as available for garbage collection, and it will be removed from memory when possible. The removal of the object is an implicit operation.

Some issues arise from garbage collection, however, particularly in the Java implementation:

Collection Times Are Unpredictable

Objects are "marked" for collection when their last reference goes out of scope, but this does not mean these objects are actually removed from memory at that time. Java implements a garbage collector that runs in a separate thread of execution along with your program, periodically checking for things to clean up. There is no guarantee if or when the collection will run.

Because this collection occurs when the collector gets around to it, it is possible that a bug-free program could repeatedly create a number of objects marked for collection but not actually removed from memory. Because the objects may not have been removed from memory yet, the program could receive an out-of-memory error when creating a new object, even though it released the last reference for all the objects it had previously created.

Java does permit you to force garbage collection as needed, but this introduces a certain amount of overhead.

Java Doesn't Implement True Destructors

Java defines a near-equivalent to a C++ destructor with its `finalize` method in a class. However, because garbage collection doesn't guarantee that the objects will actually be released, it is possible that the `finalize` method will never get called.

For C++ programmers, this means that the destructors they rely on are not so reliable in the Java language. Therefore, a more manual process, when compared to C++, is required to perform your own "close" or "shutdown" operations on an object when you are done using it in Java.

User Interface

Java provides a rich set of user interface classes for creating applications. The original set of classes was called the Abstract Windowing Toolkit, but it has been replaced for the most part by the Swing classes.

Using these classes, you can create Java applications with buttons, lists, check boxes, and other user interface elements. Although Java lacks an official standard, these classes have remained fairly compatible since the release of the 1.1 version of the Java Development Kit (JDK).

Swing also provides control over the appearance of the user interface components. This is to say that the same button running on the same computer can have several different appearances in a Java, based on the selected "look and feel."

Multiple Inheritance

Java does not support multiple inheritance. Many people argue that Java provides interfaces, which are similar, but the reality is that interfaces do not provide for reusable code. Interfaces can mimic multiple inheritance, but the programmer must still write the code for the interface in each class that specifies and implements it.

The issue with multiple inheritance revolves around whether the benefits it provides in terms of reuse offset the complexity of the "diamond problem" it creates. The complexity revolves around the confusion in a scenario where you have two classes derived from the same base class used as the multiple base classes of some new class. In this scenario, you would have two of the same ultimate base classes in your new class.

Generics/Templates

Although the current version of Java (1.4) does not support templates, as C++ does, templates will be a part of version 1.5, which may be available by the time you read this. In Java version 1.5, the feature is called *generics* instead of templates, but the result is the same: You can create generic-type-safe classes that the compiler builds for you as needed.

Some people considered the lack of templates/generics in Java version 1.4 and earlier to be a benefit, stating that the C++ implementation is too difficult to master or could lead to sloppy object designs. Although it is true that a well-designed object library or framework can mostly eliminate the need for templates/generics, as is often the case in programming, if the feature exists and it is helpful, you should use it.

Generics are considered one of the major changes to the 1.5 version of the Java language.

C#

C# (pronounced *C-sharp)* was created by Microsoft as a new programming language in late 1999/early 2000 to be released with their .NET endeavor. Its programming paradigm is very similar to Java, and much like Java, C# implements a sort of tokenized bytecode system with the promise of multiplatform compatibility. In 2000, the EMCA approved C# as a standard language at the request of Microsoft. This was an unusual thing for Microsoft, because it meant that the C# language was now a defined standard that Microsoft would not be able to alter as they might see fit. Many in the industry saw this as a benefit of C#, giving it an identity independent from Microsoft.

The theory behind C# is similar to that of Java, in that it is a language that can be used to create multiplatform programs. In practice, however, Microsoft views C# as a means of creating programs on Windows platforms. Although open-source projects exist to port the system to other platforms, their success is not guaranteed, and Microsoft has made no announcements of support for non-Windows platforms.

In Windows, a typical program is composed of a binary executable file. That is to say, the source code for the program is compiled into a machine-executable format. .NET still provides this means of software development, although it's specifically referred to as "unmanaged code."

A new model under .NET mimics the Java platform: An application called the *Common Language Runtime (CLR)* is used to interpret and execute bytecodes of instructions, tokenized from various source modules. This is identical in concept to how the Java Virtual Machine (JVM) works. The .NET CLR has two distinct differences from the JVM:

- The primary language for the CLR, C#, is now a standardized language. Whereas Sun maintains control of Java, C# is accepted by the European Computer Manufacturers Association as a standard language. This means that Microsoft cannot make changes to the language on a whim, and backward compatibility must be maintained.

  What's more, the CLR supports languages besides C#, such as C++, COBOL, and Java. Although these languages are not typically supported in their entirety, they are implemented in majority.

- The CLR supports compilation to native machine code for improved performance.

Also, like the JVM, the CLR maintains control over executing code, and has the ability to stop malicious programs. Like in Java, CLR programs tend to be slower than their machine-executable counterparts. Programs written for the CLR are referred to as "managed code."

The CLR also provides other features, such as the implementation of a standard class set and a Common Type System for implementing data types in the same manner (a "time" object is the same in C#, Managed C++, and Managed COBOL).

Reusable Code

C# contains a vast amount of reusable code, just like Java does. Using the .NET Framework classes, support for database connections, images, Internet connections, and so on are provided.

Performance: Interpreted and Compiled Code?

Like Java programs, C# programs are compiled into a tokenized "bytecode" that a separate program can understand and execute. The Common Language Runtime (CLR) is the program that works with the tokenized bytecode of C#.

The CLR actually goes beyond a "virtual machine" approach, however, and actually compiles applications on the fly to native code, thus improving their performance. In the case of web server applications called often, such as ASP.NET, the results of the compilation are cached and reused, again for better performance.

So C# goes through distinct steps: Programs written in it are first "compiled" into a CLR-compatible format (similar to what Java does), and then compiled into native machine code by the CLR the first time it is run.

C# provides native support for COM components and the Windows API, as well as restricted use of native pointers. This means, though the language may not be as fast as a direct executable application (because of CLR interpretation), performance will typically not be as poor as that experienced by Java applications.

Security

C# implements security control like Java in a sandbox format, but the basic control is set up by an *assembly,* which helps define the operations a particular program or class is allowed to perform.

Unlike Java however, C# does support pointers to directly operate on memory, although their usage can be controlled by security settings.

Portability

C# is theoretically portable, but no non-Microsoft operating systems currently can use it. This is not to say it is completely nonportable, however. Microsoft also has the handheld operating system currently called "Windows Mobile" (formerly Windows CE, Windows PocketPC, PocketPC 2000, and so on), which is distributed with the .NET Framework and the CLR needed to execute C# compiled programs.

As with Java, C# can be used on web servers, desktops, and handheld devices, as long as they are running the appropriate version of Windows.

Garbage Collection

Like Java, C# implements automatic garbage collection. Although destructors can be declared in C#, it is important to note that they are called when the garbage collector determines an object is no longer reachable by code and when memory space is needed.

Destructors have the same format in C# as in C++:

```
~ClassName();
```

The garbage collector will invoke this method automatically, when it sees fit.

In the event you are handling nonmanaged (non-CLR) resources, you may want to force the garbage collection for the object. In order to do this, you must declare your class to implement the Idisposable interface, and you must also provide a Dispose method. A typical example follows:

```
using System;
class Testing : Idisposable
{
    bool is_disposed = false;
    protected virtual void Dispose(bool disposing)
    {
        if (!is_disposed) // only dispose once!
        {
            if (disposing)
            {
                // Not in destructor, OK to reference other objects
            }
            // perform cleanup for this object
        }
        this.is_disposed = true;
    }
    public void Dispose()
    {
```

```
        Dispose(true);
        // tell the GC not to finalize
        GC.SuppressFinalize(this);
    }
    ~Testing()
    {
        Dispose(false);
    }
}
```

User Interface

C# does provide rich user interface support, but C# is limited to the Windows operating. C# also provides the ability to use existing ActiveX controls in a simple manner.

Like Java and its JavaBeans, the C# language was designed to facilitate easily creating components or add-ons that can be tied to the IDE used to develop programs. This means that you can easily create new controls of your own design and quickly and easily use them as a native part of the IDE's component gallery.

Multiple Inheritance

C# does not support multiple inheritance as C++ does. It does support interfaces, however, in a fashion similar to Java. As with Java, interfaces define code that must be written, not code that is reused.

Generics/Templates

C# does not provide support for templates or generics as C++ and Java 1.5 do.

Assemblies

An *assembly* implements the set of information for one or more of the code files shown in Table 12-2.

Assembly	Description
Versioning	Groups modules that should have the same version information.
Deployment	Groups code modules and resources that support your model of deployment.

Table 12-2   Assembly Implementations

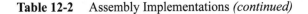

Assembly	Description
Reuse	Groups modules if they can be logically used together for some purpose. For example, an assembly consisting of types and classes used infrequently for program maintenance can be put in the same assembly. In addition, types that you intend to share with multiple applications should be grouped into an assembly, and the assembly should be signed with a strong name.
Security	Groups modules containing types that require the same security permissions.
Scoping	Groups modules containing types whose visibility should be restricted to the same assembly.

Table 12-2   Assembly Implementations *(continued)*

Assemblies are nothing more than text files similar to source code. They can be embedded within a CLR-executable program or defined outside the CLR for multiple files. Many programs can include an assembly in the single executable files. The following is a brief example of an assembly for a C# project:

```
using System.Reflection;
using System.Runtime.CompilerServices;
[assembly: AssemblyTitle("")]
[assembly: AssemblyDescription("")]
[assembly: AssemblyConfiguration("")]
[assembly: AssemblyCompany("")]
[assembly: AssemblyProduct("")]
[assembly: AssemblyCopyright("")]
[assembly: AssemblyTrademark("")]
[assembly: AssemblyCulture("")]
[assembly: AssemblyVersion("1.0.*")]
[assembly: AssemblyDelaySign(false)]
[assembly: AssemblyKeyFile("")]
[assembly: AssemblyKeyName("")]
```

Quiz

1. How was the ENIAC originally programmed?

2. What are the two contributions of Grace Hopper?

3. What is the importance of the EDSAC system?

4. What was the first modern programming language?

5. What is Dennis Ritchie's contribution to programming?

6. What is Bjarne Stroustrup's contribution to programming?

7. Why is C/C++ considered a high-performance programming language?

8. What was the original purpose of the Java programming language?

9. What is the Java Virtual Machine?

10. What is the primary weakness of the C# programming language?

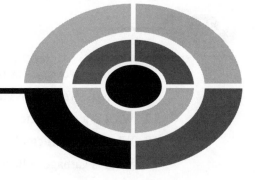

Final Exam

1. What is a class?

2. What is an object?

3. Define what an attribute or property of an object is.

4. Define what an object behavior is.

5. Describe the methods and attributes of a Card class to represent a card used in card games.

6. Define inheritance.

7. Describe the benefits of inheritance.

8. Which of these is a base class: Vehicle or Minivan?

9. Which is an example of inheritance: an Engine class and a Diesel class, or an Engine class and a Car class?

10. What is a business object?

11. What is a characteristic?

12. What is a class definition?

13. What is an argument list?

14. What is a return value?

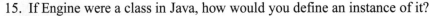

15. If Engine were a class in Java, how would you define an instance of it?

16. If Engine were a class in C++, how would you define an instance of it?

17. What is a constructor?

18. What is a destructor?

19. What is garbage collection?

20. How do you access members of an object?

21. Define encapsulation.

22. Define polymorphism.

23. Define overloading.

24. Define binding.

25. Define runtime polymorphism.

26. What is a virtual function?

27. How would you define a virtual method in C++?

28. How would you define a virtual method in Java and C#?

29. Define method overloading.

30. Compare Public, Protected, and Private members of a class.

31. Define simple inheritance.

32. Define multiple inheritance.

33. What is the "Diamond Problem" of multiple inheritance?

34. Define level inheritance.

35. What is the maximum number of levels for level inheritance?

36. What are the terms typically used to refer to the parent and child classes in C++ and Java?

37. Define abstraction.

38. What is the difference between functionality and function?

39. What is an abstract method?

40. Define an abstract class.

41. What is data decomposition?

42. What is an iconic description?

43. Define pseudo code.

44. What is an entity?

45. What is an entity relationship?

46. What is a many-to-many relationship?

47. Define a leveling diagram.

48. What is a class diagram?

49. What is an internal model?

50. What is an external model?

51. What is the "is a" test?

52. What is the "has a" test?

53. Define collaboration.

54. What is UML?

55. What is a sequence diagram?

56. What is a collaboration diagram?

57. What is a message?

58. What is association?

59. What is self-collaboration?

60. What is a Class Responsibility Collaborator diagram?

61. What is an actor?

62. What is an SME?

63. What is an Essential Use Case?

64. What is a System Case?

65. What are business rules?

66. What is a User Interface diagram?

67. What is a User Interface-Flow diagram?

68. What is a Change Case?

69. What is an interface?

70. Describe some of the basic units of project management.

71. Describe three common errors when using abstraction.

72. What is a framework?

73. Describe three basic categories of reuse.

74. How are approaches to OO programming analogous to nouns and verbs?

75. How can a hierarchy be morphed?

76. When might you use multiple inheritance?

77. What is early binding?

78. What is late binding?

79. Do UML sequence diagrams show flow control?

80. What is a finalize method in Java?

81. What is the difference between static and non-static class members?

82. What is the Java syntax to declare class Derived from class Base?

83. What is the C++ syntax to declare class Derived from class Base?

84. What is the C# syntax to declare class Derived from class Base?

85. What does the final keyword in Java mean when applied to a class?

86. Is Java a compiled or interpreted language?

87. Is C++ a compiled or interpreted language?

88. Is C# a compiled or interpreted language?

89. Which language supports multiple inheritance: Java, C++, or C#?

90. Which language offers the best portability to other platforms: Java, C++, or C#?

91. Describe one advantage and disadvantage of garbage collection.

92. Which language provides the easiest access directly to memory?

93. Which languages support interfaces syntactically: Java, C++, or C#?

94. Which languages support templates or generics: Java, C++, or C#?

95. What are the three editions of Java?

96. What is the JVM?

97. What is the CLR?

98. What has the smallest footprint, memory-wise: Java, C++, or C#?

99. What was one of the first stored-program computer systems?

100. Where did the term "bug" come from?

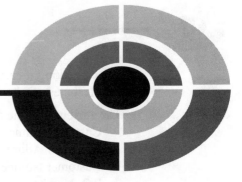

Answers to Quizzes and Final Exam

Chapter 1

1. An object is a person, place, thing, concept, or possibly event.

2. An attribute is a characteristic of an object.

3. A behavior is an action that an object is capable of performing.

4. Focusing on objects makes it easy for us to understand complex things. Objects enable us to look at details that are of interest to us and ignore other details that we are not interested in.

5. Inheritance is a way for one object to receive attributes and behaviors of another object in what programmers call an "is a" relationship.

6. Attributes and behaviors need to be defined in one object, such as Person. Other objects that require those attributes and behaviors—such as Student, Teacher, Department Chair, Dean, Secretary, and Bursar—can inherit the object. This allows for attributes and behaviors to be defined in only one

object, making it easy to add new attributes and behaviors or remove existing attributes and behaviors.

7. The attributes of the order form in Figure 1-1 are as follows:
   - Customer Name
   - Customer Address
   - Customer Number
   - P.O. Number
   - Date Shipped
   - Shipped Via
   - Required Date
   - Terms
   - Quantity
   - Item ID
   - Item Name
   - Unit Price
   - Amount
   - Subtotal
   - Sales Tax
   - Shipping & Handling
   - Total Due

8. The behaviors of the order form in Figure 1-1 are as follows:
   - Enter order information
   - Modify order information
   - Delete order
   - Process order
   - Look up order

9. These are common objects that inherit a `Person` object:
   - Student
   - Instructor
   - Dean
   - President
   - Board of Trustees
   - Security Manager
   - Security Guard
   - Bookstore Manager
   - Sales Assistant
   - Department Chair
   - Bursar
   - Registrar

- Maintenance Manager
- Maintenance Worker
- Secretary

10. See Figure B-1.

Chapter 2

1. An instance variable is an attribute of a class.

2. You determine the class size by adding the size of all its attributes.

3. You declare an instance of a class by first reserving memory for the class using the new operator followed by the constructor of the class (new RegistrationForm()). Next, declare a reference to the class and give that reference a name (RegistrationForm myRegistrationform). Finally, assign a reference to the memory reserved for the class to the reference using an assignment statement.

4. An instance variable is declared by specifying the data type of the variable, followed by the variable name, and ending with a semicolon within the body of a class definition.

5. A data type is a keyword that tells the computer the kind of data you want to store in a memory location.

6. A method definition consists of the name of a method, an argument list (if any), the data type of the value returned by the method, and the method body.

7. Although some programmers consider an argument list and a parameter list to be the same thing, other programmers consider a parameter list to be values passed to a method when the method is called, and they consider an argument list to be values defined within the method definition that receive values passed to the method.

Figure B-1   The relationship between the Person object and objects that are persons

8. A member method is called by first declaring an instance of a class and then using the name of the instance followed by the dot operator and the name of the method—`myInstance.myMethod()`, for example.

9. A constructor is a method of a class that is called automatically when an instance of a class is declared. A constructor is defined in the class and must have the same name as the class name. A class can have multiple constructors, each with a different argument list. The argument list is traditionally used with the constructor to initialize instance variables of the class.

10. An instance variable is accessed by first declaring an instance of a class and then using the name of the instance followed by the dot operator and the name of the variable—`myInstance.myVariable`, for example.

Chapter 3

1. Encapsulation is a technique of linking together attributes and procedures to form an object.

2. Encapsulation enables a programmer to institute "checks and balances" by placing attributes and procedures in a class and then defining rules in the class to control its access.

3. An access specifier is a programming language keyword that tells the computer what part of the application can access data and functions/methods defined within the access specifier.

4. The public access specifier determines attributes and procedures that are accessible by using an instance of the class.

5. The private access specifier identifies attributes and procedures that are only accessible by a procedure that is defined by the class.

6. The protected access specifier stipulates attributes and procedures that can be inherited and used by another class.

7. A subclass inherits public and protected portions of the super class.

8. In C++, access specifiers define a section of a class that contains attributes and member functions. In Java, each attribute and member method contains the access specifier.

9. A super class cannot access any portion of a subclass.

10. Programmers require that some attributes of a class be accessed only by a member procedure in order to validate values assigned to attributes. A programmer who wants access to some attributes calls a member procedure, which applies any validation rules before assigning values to attributes.

Chapter 4

1. Polymorphism technically means that one thing has the ability to take many shapes. In programming terms, the "thing" is the name of a method and the "shape" is the behavior performed by the method.

2. Polymorphism is implemented by overloading a method or by using virtual functions.

3. Late binding is the binding of a method call to a method definition and is performed at run time if some information is missing at compile time that is known only when the application runs.

4. Early binding is the binding of a method call to a method definition and is performed at compile time if all the information is available at compile time.

5. The advantage of run-time polymorphism is that a program can respond to events that occur during execution.

6. The advantage of compile-time polymorphism is that no time is lost in binding when the program runs because binding is completed when the executable program is created.

7. An interface specifies a standard method name, argument list, return value, and behavior. Programmers who develop classes and methods define methods that adhere to an interface.

8. Polymorphism permits an interface to be defined as a set of standard methods and behaviors by using overloaded methods and virtual methods.

9. A virtual function is a placeholder for the real function that is defined when the programming is running.

10. Overloading is a technique for implementing polymorphism by defining two or more methods with the same name but different argument lists.

Chapter 5

1. Inheritance is a programming technique that enables a class to inherit some or all attributes and behaviors of another class.

2. Simple inheritance is a type of inheritance in which a class inherits from just one class.

3. Level inheritance is a type of inheritance in which two or more levels of inheritance exist. Each level consists of a parent-child relationship whereby the child of the middle level is also the parent of the lower level. The last child in level inheritance inherits directly and indirectly from other levels.

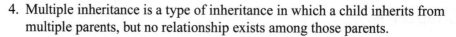

4. Multiple inheritance is a type of inheritance in which a child inherits from multiple parents, but no relationship exists among those parents.

5. The "is a" test is given to determine if a child "is a" parent. For example, is a graduate student a student? If so, the child (graduate student) can inherit from the parent (student). If not, the child cannot inherit from the parent.

6. Multiple inheritance should be used whenever a child needs to inherit attributes and behaviors from parents that are not related to each other.

7. Level inheritance should be used whenever a child needs to inherit attributes and behaviors from parents that are related to each other.

8. There is no maximum number of levels in level inheritance. However, you should use no more than three levels; otherwise, you run the risk that the levels will become unmanageable.

9. A child can inherit public and protected members of a parent class.

10. Base class is the term used in C++ to refer to a parent class. Derived class is the C++ term for a child class. A super class is Java's parent class, and Java's child class is called a subclass.

Chapter 6

1. Abstraction is a way for the programmer of a super class to require the programmer of a subclass to define a method.

2. Abstraction should be used in a program when there isn't any way to define a good default method in the super class.

3. An abstract method is a method defined in a super class that must be redefined in a subclass that inherits the super class.

4. An abstract method cannot be called within a program.

5. A compiler error occurs if an abstract method is not redefined.

6. An instance of an abstract class cannot be declared in a program.

7. An abstract method cannot be called directly by a subclass.

8. A programmer of a subclass that inherits an abstract super class must redefine the abstract methods defined in the subclass, even if those methods are not called within the application.

9. A super class can contain a mixture of abstract methods and non-abstract methods.

10. Only abstract methods must be redefined in a subclass that inherits from the abstract super class.

Chapter 7

1. An attribute is information used to describe an object, whereas data is the smallest amount of information used to describe an object. For example, a student name is an attribute, and a student's first name and last name are data.

2. A leveling diagram is used to simplify the understanding of a complex application. The first level of the leveling diagram provides a simplified overview of the application, and subsequent levels provide a progressively more detailed view of the application.

3. Entity is another term used for "object."

4. The purpose of using an entity relationship diagram is to illustrate the functional relationship between two or more entities that are not hierarchically related to each other.

5. 0:N is a ratio used in an entity relationship diagram to define a relationship. For example, 0:N in a student course relationship means that a student doesn't have to register for any course and could register for many courses.

6. Decomposing an attribute is the process of reducing an attribute to data.

7. A processing model is a diagram that illustrates the steps in a behavior of an object.

8. Pseudo code is a textual description of a behavior that uses a combination of English words and programming language syntax.

9. A class diagram is an illustration that describes a class, its attributes, and its behaviors.

10. A many-to-one relationship defines the relationship between two entities where there are many instances of one entity to one instance of another. For example, many students are in one course.

Chapter 8

1. Many object-oriented applications store data in a relational database and use a conversion routine to translate data from data members of objects into rows in a relational database and to transfer data from a relational database to data members of objects.

2. Objects are thought of as nouns, such as a person, place, or thing. Tasks are thought of as verbs because they describe actions within an application.

3. Some business applications cannot be organized easily into discrete objects, which posses a challenge for programmers.

4. A dynamic hierarchy is an organization of objects in which the relationship among the objects is changed over a short timeframe.

5. A static hierarchy is an organization of objects in which the relationship among objects is maintained over time.

6. A hierarchy is morphed when a member function has many versions of a behavior requiring many overloaded functions.

7. Some programmers feel we view the world as tasks rather than as objects. For example, we think to turn on the air conditioner in hot weather, which is a task. We don't think air conditioner, turn on, which is the object-oriented logical approach.

8. Object-oriented programming theory assumes that the real world is organized neatly into objects that can be defined easily as objects in an object-oriented application. Some aspects of the real world can be defined as objects; other aspects of the real world don't lend themselves to such a definition.

9. Yes, the goal of an object-oriented program is to simulate real-world objects in a computer application. However, many business applications do not simulate real-world business situations. The reality is that simulating the real world does not necessarily use the best possible means to achieve a business objective.

10. An internal model describes how an application works behind the scenes. An external model describes how a person interacts with the application.

Chapter 9

1. Collaboration describes how two or more classes interact and work with one another.

2. A UML (Unified Modeling Language) sequence diagram is used to represent a sequence of operations between classes.

3. No. They are typically diagrams of smaller portions or overviews of an application. An application may contain many sequence diagrams.

4. No. Unlike flow charts, sequence diagrams do not show flow control; they show sequence.

5. A return value from a method call.

6. A method call from one object to the other, as indicated by an arrow.

7. A UML collaboration diagram shows the basic collaboration or relationship between classes.

8. A message is normally a method call. A class may receive a message by having one of its methods called, or it may send a message to another class by invoking a method of the other class.

9. No. If you have a class derived from another, for diagram purposes, it is best to use the more descriptive derived class name even if none of the derived class methods are used (in other words, use `Enrollments`, not `Vector`).

10. It is a diagram that shows the class name, its methods, and the classes with which it collaborates. A CRC diagram provides an overview of how a class interacts with other classes and what it provides. It is not concerned with sequences or detailed collaboration descriptions.

Chapter 10

1. An actor is a person, organization, or thing that might interact with a system.

2. A subject matter expert (SME) is a person who has expert knowledge of the system but may not use the system.

3. You should request that they have ready any sample reports or forms that they currently use to do their job.

4. Ask the most important questions first, in case you run out of time.

5. An essential use case is a nontechnical view of how your system will work with its users.

6. The purpose of the use case diagram is simply to identify the use of the system, not its technical details.

7. The system use case defines the technical aspect of the system.

8. Business rules define the rules a business must follow, and they must be incorporated into the system.

9. User interface flow diagramming lets you define the flow of the program, from a menu selection to a specific form.

10. An actor class is a class that represents an actor within a system.

Chapter 11

1. An interface specifies what a class must do, but not how it does it. It is syntactically similar to a class, but its methods are declared without any body. A class implements an interface by creating a complete set of methods defined by the interface.

2. An interface diagram shows how a class can implement an interface.

3. An interface is used in a program to enable similar classes to have a standard behavior while having the programmer who builds these classes define how the behavior is performed.

4. The purpose of a user interface is to enable a user to use a program. An interface is a standard behavior. Programmers who use a class that implements an interface can expect that the class will define a set of standard methods. Programmers who build classes for use by other programmers must define a set of standard methods that conform to a standard interface.

5. The C programming language doesn't use an interface because C is not an object-oriented programming language.

6. An interface is similar to multiple inheritance.

7. C++ does not support an interface, but it does support multiple inheritance.

8. Java and C# support interfaces because they do not support multiple inheritance.

9. A component is a class designed to fit into some preexisting class framework and may do so through inheritance or by implementing one or more interfaces. However, it must follow its environment's rules for components.

10. An Integrated Development Environment is a good example because it enables programmers to drag and drop components such as buttons from a tool palette onto a form.

Chapter 12

1. The ENIAC was programmed by rewiring the computer.

2. Grace Hopper coined the term *bug* and helped developed the COBOL programming language.

3. The EDSAC system is commonly thought of as the first stored-program system.

4. FORTRAN was the first modern programming language.

5. Dennis Ritchie created the C programming language.

6. Bjarne Stroustrup created the C++ programming language.

7. C/C++ is considered a high-performance programming language because it lets you directly manipulate memory.

8. The Java programming language was originally intended to program smart devices such as cable television boxes.

9. The Java Virtual Machine is a program running on a computer that interprets the "tokenized" source code of a Java program and executes it.

10. The primary weakness of the C# programming language is that there is no guarantee C# will be supported for non-Windows platforms. Microsoft, who created C#, views C# as a means of creating programs on Windows platforms.

Answers to Final Exam

1. A class is a set of methods and data items combined in a single entity. It provides some service or does some work and serves as a functionality package.

2. An object is an instance of a class. A class is essentially a data type, and an object is a variable of that data type.

3. An attribute or property is a piece of data in a class. It has a value at any given time and may be readable, writable, or both.

4. Object behavior defines how an object works under certain operations.

5. Attibutes: Suit, Value, FaceUp
   Methods: GetSuit, SetSuit, GetValue, SetValue, IsFaceUp, Flip

6. Inheritance means that a class is based upon the methods and attributes of an existing class.

7. Code reuse

8. Vehicle, because a minivan "is a" vehicle—the minivan is derived from vehicle.

9. Engine and Diesel, because Diesel "is a" type of engine. A Car "has a(n)" engine, which describes containment, not inheritance.

10. A business object is a class used by a business system or application, such as an order form.

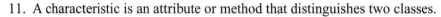
11. A characteristic is an attribute or method that distinguishes two classes.

12. A class definition defines attributes and methods that are members of the class.

13. An argument list is a list of data items passed to a method or function for it to do its job.

14. A return value is a value that a method returns as its output or result. Return values are optional.

15. `Engine anEngine = new Engine();`

16. `Engine anEngine;`

17. A constructor is a special method that initializes the attributes of a class.

18. A destructor is a special method that releases any resources (such as memory) from an object instance. Java does not implement "true" destructors, while C++ does because Java performs garbage collection while C++ doesn't (and garbage collection is not guaranteed to run before the program terminates).

19. Garbage collection is the ability of a language to automatically remove objects created in memory when the last reference or use of the object goes out of scope or is no longer needed.

20. In Java, C++, and C#, you use the dot (.) operator. C++ also uses the arrow (->) operator if you have a pointer to an object.

21. Encapsulation is the grouping of concepts or behaviors into a class. It defines how the class behaves, without offering details as to how it implements that behavior.

22. Polymorphism means that something has many shapes and that something is a method of an object-oriented programming language. In programming terms, a *thing* is the name of a method and a *shape* is the behavior performed by a method. Polymorphism means that one or more methods with the same name exist for many behaviors.

23. Overloading is another one of those terms you hear used in conjunction with polymorphism. Overloading means that two or more methods are defined using the same name, but with different argument list.

24. Binding is the association of a method definition (or function body) with a call to a method, and occurs either at compile time or at runtime. Compile-time or Early binding is used for normal method calls. No time is lost when the program runs because binding is completed when the executable program is created. Runtime or Late binding is implemented using a virtual function, which uses a base reference to point to the type of object that contains the correct method definition.

25. Run-time polymorphism uses virtual functions to create a standard interface and to call the underlying functions. Those function definitions are bound to function calls during run time.

26. A virtual function is used to trick the computer into thinking a function is defined, but the function doesn't have to be defined at that moment. Instead, the virtual function can be a placeholder for the real function that is defined in a program. Virtual functions help support run-time polymorphism.

27. Use the keyword `virtual` in the declaration of the method, such as `Foo`:

```
class Boo {
public:
virtual void Foo();
};
```

28. Methods are virtual in Java and C# by default. To create a virtual method without any body in these languages, use the `abstract` keyword in the declaration of the method.

29. Method Overloading is a technique to implement polymorphism by defining two or more methods with the same name but different argument list.

30. Public members are seen by all methods, even ones outside the class. Protected members are seen only to that class and ones derived from it. Private members are seen only by that class, and nothing else.

31. Simple inheritance occurs when there is one parent-child relationship—that is, one child inherits from one parent.

32. Multiple inheritance is where there is a multiple parent-child relationship. The child inherits from more than one parent. Java and C# do not support multiple inheritance, but C++ does.

33. It describes a situation where a single base class (such as `Person`) contains a data member such as `Name`, and then two classes are derived from it such as `Student` and `Instructor`. Now that `Student` and `Instructor` contain a `Name` member, if we were to create a new class derived from both (such as a TeachingAssistant class), then the object could have two names for what is really one person.

34. Level inheritance happens when a child inherits from a parent and then becomes a parent itself to a child.

35. There is no practical limit—if you find a compiler that can't handle 1,000 levels of inheritance, the real problem is that you have a poor design because there are too many levels of inheritance. A rule of thumb is to try and limit things to three levels.

36. C++ typically uses the terms base class and derived class, while Java typically uses super class and subclass.

37. Abstraction is a way a programmer of a super class forces a programmer of a subclass to define a behavior.

38. Programmers distinguish a behavior from instructions used to perform the behavior using the term's functionality and function.

39. An abstract method does not provide a method body. A class with an abstract method requires derived classes to implement the method body. A class with an abstract method is called an abstract class. Abstract methods are called "pure virtual" methods in C++.

40. An abstract class is one that has one or more abstract methods. Because of this, you cannot instantiate an object of this type. You must create a derived class that provides the method bodies for the abstract methods, and then you can instantiate the derived class.

41. Object-oriented programmers decompose each attribute into data and then use data in the corresponding class definition to describe the object. Decomposition is the technique that reduces an attribute into its data components.

42. An iconic description is a graphic picture of the process. Textual description describes the process in words.

43. Pseudo code is a combination of English words and programming language syntax that describe in words how a process works. The result is not entirely English, nor a syntactically correct program. It's used to enforce understanding and requirements without actually writing a program.

44. An entity refers to an individual item, and may be a single piece of data or an object.

45. Entity relationship (or functional relationship) describes how objects are related or interact with one another.

46. It defines a relationship between two different types (such as Student and Course) where any single first type (Student) can be related to 1 or more of the second type (Course), and vice versa. For example, one student may be registered in many courses, and a course may have many students.

47. A leveling diagram depicts an application in layers where the top level has the least amount of detail and is the easiest to understand. Subsequent levels have more detail and are usually the hardest to understand.

48. A class diagram is an illustration that describes a class, its attributes, and its behaviors.

49. The internal model describes how an application works behind the scenes.

50. The external model describes how a person interacts with the application.

51. The "is a" test asks the question is object A a type of object B. If so, then object A can inherit object B. For example, a Minivan is a type of Vehicle, so Minivan can be derived from Vehicle.

52. The "has a" test asks the question does object A have an object B. If so, then object A would have a data member of type Object B. For example, a Vehicle has an Engine, so a Vehicle object would have an Engine object as a data member.

53. Collaboration occurs when two or more things work together or cooperate with each other in order to achieve a common goal. In programming, it means that one class might have methods that call methods from another class.

54. UML stands for Unified Modeling Language, and is a set of diagramming and text standard to help define a process and classes involved in the process.

55. A Sequence diagram is a diagram that shows the typical sequence of events for a process.

56. Collaboration diagrams are used to display basic interaction between classes.

57. When discussing collaboration, we typically say that a class collaborates with another via a Message. Technically, a message is a function call, so if we say that class A sends a message to class B, we are saying that class A is calling a method in a class B object.

58. Association means that the two classes need to know how to interact with one another, and is part of the description of collaboration.

59. Self-collaboration is when a class invokes its own methods.

60. The Class Responsibility Collaborator (CRC) diagram is intended to be an all-inclusive list of how a single class is to be designed. A CRC diagram lists the class name at the top, and then two columns below for responsibilities and collaborators.

61. An actor is a person, organization, or anything that might interact with a system. Actors don't need to be persons. If a system needs to output a file in a certain format for a government agency, then that agency might be considered an actor as well.

62. An SME (Subject Matter Expert) is a person who has intimate knowledge about the work or process for which you are developing a system. They don't need to have any computer experience.

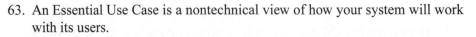
63. An Essential Use Case is a nontechnical view of how your system will work with its users.

64. A System Use Case defines the technical view of how your system will work.

65. Business Rules are the rules and laws that govern how a business operates. An SME is typically the most accurate source of business rules.

66. User Interface Diagrams are prototypes or designs for a programs user interface. It may contain forms and controls, as well as menu items.

67. User Interface-Flow diagrams let you define the flow of the program in terms of the user interface, such as the steps a user must take to perform some process.

68. A Change case represents possible or definite changes to a system. The goal of the change case is to design a flexible system and anticipate possible or definite changes so that the system can be designed to be easily adaptable.

69. An interface represents a set of standard methods to provide some behavior or feature to a class. For a class to have some certain behavior, it declares that it will implement the interface that defines the behavior.

70. Client—Entity for which the work is being done.

    Project—The definition of the project and the group for the remaining items. Clients can have multiple projects.

    Work Request—Identifies a request, feature, change, or bug report. Projects are made up of requests and features initially, and then as time goes on features, changes, and bug reports are added.

    Task—The work performed by the entity developing the project. Tasks are the work performed to complete a Work Request.

71. Failure of a programmer to define an abstract method in a subclass, an attempt by the programmer to call the super class's abstract method, and an attempt to declare an instance of the abstract super class in the program.

72. A framework is a set of classes or class library that has been designed to work well together and that follows a certain paradigm.

73. Objects that are very reusable across different applications (like a string class or stream hierarchy), objects that are reusable within a particular set of programs (like a student class and hierarchy for academic institution programs), and objects that simply will never be reused again anywhere.

74. Objects are thought of as nouns (person, place, or thing). Tasks are thought of as verbs because they describe action within an application.

75. A hierarchy is morphed when a member function has many versions of a behavior requiring many overloaded functions.

76. Multiple inheritance should be used whenever a child needs to inherit attributes and behaviors from parents that are not related to each other.

77. Early binding is the binding of a method call to a method definition and is performed at compile time if all the information is available at compile time.

78. Late binding is the binding of a method call to a method definition and is performed at run time. It implicitly makes use of base class pointers or references to derived objects, and methods must be virtual.

79. No. Unlike flow charts, Sequence diagrams do not show flow control; they show sequence.

80. It represents the pseudo-destructor for a class. If garbage is collected, the finalize method is called, but there is no guarantee when or even if this will occur.

81. Nonstatic data members occur in each instance of the class and nonstatic methods can work with them as well as static methods. Static data members occur only once no matter how many instances of a class and static methods can only work directly with static data members. You do not need to declare an instance of a class to use its static methods or properties.

82. `public class Derived extends Base { ...`

83. `class Derived : public Base { ...` // public may also be private or protected.

84. `class Derived : Base { ...`

85. It means that no class can be derived from it.

86. It is compiled into bytecode, and then the Java Virtual Machine interprets the byte code.

87. It is compiled into native machine code.

88. It is compiled into byte code, and then the CLR recompiles it into native machine code.

89. C++

90. Java, since its bytecode can be used without recompiling. C# and the CLR are designed for this ability, but only currently available on Windows Desktop and Windows Mobile operating systems.

91. Garbage collection releases the programming from the task of manually releasing memory. The disadvantage is that garbage collection systems are unpredictable as to when they release memory and may require manual coding to do so.

92. C++, which supports pointers directly to memory. C# includes some support for memory access and Java provides none.

93. Java and C#. C++ can mimic this behavior by defining an abstract class and using multiple inheritance.

94. C++ and Java version 1.5

95. J2EE—Java Enterprise Edition for servers, J2SE—Java Standard Edition for desktops, and J2ME—Java Micro Edition for handheld devices.

96. The JVM, or Java Virtual Machine, is the program that must be installed on a computer in order to interpret and execute the compiled byte code of a Java program.

97. The CLR, or Common Language Runtime, is the program that must be installed on a computer in order to interpret and compile the bytecode generated by compiling a C# program.

98. C++, because it doesn't require a JVM or CLR to be in memory while it runs.

99. ENIAC, built in the mid-1940s

100. Grace Hopper coined the term when she found a moth stuck between some tubes, which was causing her program to act incorrectly.

Classes in Java

Creating a new class in Java requires the use of the `class` keyword:

Modifier class ClassName [extends SuperClass] [implements Interface] { }

If a class is defined as part of a package, then its full name is `package-name.classname`. If it is not in a package, then the full name is `classname`. This information is important for instantiating and using classes that have already been defined (by Sun or a third party).

The *Modifier* may be one or more of the following:

Modifier	Meaning
Public	The class can be accessed by any other class, even outside its package (if it has one). If left off, then only classes in the same package can access the class.
Final	The class cannot be subclassed (derived from). A class with any `final` member functions is not required to be considered `final` itself.
Abstract	The class cannot be instantiated, and must be used as a super class (base class). If a class defines any `abstract` members, it should also be declared abstract itself. Mutually exclusive with `final`.

Extends

The keyword `extends` means that the new class is derived from another class, mentioned after the `extends` keyword. If the new class is termed a subclass, its base class is termed a super class. If the super class is an abstract class, then the new class must implement any required `abstract` methods for it to be instantiated.

Implements

The `implements` keyword means the new class will provide the required functions to implement an interface. See "Interfaces" for additional information.

Fields and Member Functions

Classes have fields (or members) that describe an object. Fields are defined as a list of data declarations of either fundamental and/or class type. A field data member is declared in the following manner:

Modifier DataType MemberName, MemberName2;

A member function is declared in the following manner:

Modifier Datatype MemberName([ParamList]);

The modifiers for each field are the following:

Modifier	Meaning
public	Other classes can access the field.
private	The field cannot be accessed outside of the class.
protected	The field can be accessed by the class that defines it, and its subclasses.
abstract	You're giving the signature of the method (declaring it as a member) but giving no implementation of the method. All nonabstract classes that derive from the class containing one or more abstract methods must implement all abstract methods. Does not apply to data fields.
final	**For data members** The field must be given an initial value in the declaration; the value can't be changed later (similar to a const in C++). **For function members** The function cannot be overridden or defined in subclasses. The body of the function must be declared.

Modifier	Meaning
static	**For data members** The field does not require an object instance for access. Member is not created per instance but per class. **For function members** The function can be invoked without instantiating an object. The functions have no "this" reference.

The following example shows a simple class with a couple of simple fields: one is the intrinsic, int, and the other is a special class, String (that is usually instantiated via new).

```
public class OurApplet
{
 public int xPosition;
 private String author;
}
```

Data members can be initialized optionally in the same line in which they are declared. An alternative means to declare and initialize the data members in the above class might be

```
public class OurApplet
{
 public int xPosition=0;
 private String author="Mario";
}
```

Methods

Classes use methods to communicate with other objects. Methods allow you to set or get information about the current state of the object. This type of implementation encapsulates the data for the class. In the preceding example class, you would want the class to support methods to get and set the xPosition and String fields within the class.

Like classes and fields, methods also have modifiers (public, private, and so on) that describe the scope of the method. When a method is final, it means subclasses can't override or hide the method.

Methods can return one value. This means that you can write a Get type of method that returns the xPosition, or you can return an error value. Consider the following code that implements a couple of simple methods—getPosition and putPosition—on the class just shown, OurApplet:

```
public class OurApplet
{
```

```
private int xPosition;
String author;
public OurApplet () { // a Constructor
  xPosition = 0;
}
public void putPosition(int x) {
 xPosition = x;
}
public int getPosition() {
 return xPosition;
}
}
```

Constructors

A constructor is a function within a class that has the same name as the class and no return type, which is automatically used to initialize the object. When you call new to instantiate a new object, the constructor for that class instance is invoked. As with other functions, constructors can be overloaded.

```
Public class OurPoint {
     Private int xPosition, yPosition;
     OurPoint() {
             yPosition = 0;
             xPosition = 0;}
     OurPoint( int X, int Y ) {
             yPosition = X;
             xPosition = Y;
}
```

Here's a sample:

```
OurPoint P = new OurPoint( 4, 5 ); // Invoke second constructor
```

Subclasses may invoke their super class constructors specifically, using the super keyword. The constructor is the only function permitted to use the super keyword. The format is

```
Public class SomeClass extends SomeSuperClass {
     SomeClass( int X ) // Constructor
     {
             super(x); // Invoke Super class constructor,
that accepts an integer.
```

Finalizers

Some languages implement a `destructor` function, which like the constructor is automatically invoked. Destructors, however, are invoked when the object goes out of scope. Java does not implement destructors, but does provide a special function called `finalize`, which performs a similar task.

In Java, because of garbage collection, there is no guarantee as to when an object will be released, or if it will be released at all. There are various methods to manually invoke garbage collection (such as `System.gc()`), but the fact that normal execution may not invoke a finalizer is the reason that destructors are not supported.

Finalizers are used to release system resources, such as an open file or socket handle, used by a class. Finalizers can not be overridden, and they always have the same signature:

```
Protected void finalize() {
}
```

Static and Nonstatic Initializers

In addition to autoinitialization and constructors, classes may define a static initializer and nonstatic initializer section. These initializers are used when initialization of a data member requires more than a simple, single, line of code. They are declared like functions inside the class with { and } to denote the code section, but with no function name.

Static initializers are run when the class is loaded by the classLoader the first time. Nonstatic initializers are run when each instance of a new object is created.

```
Public class Foo {
    public static int si;
    public int i;

    static {       // Static Initializer
        si = 1;
    }
    {        // Nonstatic Initializer
        i = 2;
    }
```

Interfaces

An interface can contain one or more member functions of constant declarations, and in some ways is similar to an `abstract` super class. Interfaces differ from abstract classes in the following manner:

- An interface cannot implement any member functions, while an `abstract` class can.
- A class can implement many interfaces, but have only one super class.
- An interface is not part of any hierarchy.
- Interfaces can be modified after being used as a super class for other interfaces, but it is strongly recommended not to.

Defining an interface requires use of the `interface` keyword—for example:

```
Modifier interface InterfaceName extends SuperClassName
{
     // Member function signatures (bodies are not defined)
     // Constant declarations
}
```

Interface *Modifiers* may only be public and/or abstract. Their definition is similar to that of the `class` keyword. The `abstract` keyword is implicit, and should not be used in newer Java programs.

An example of an interface is as follows:

```
public interface Securable {
     boolean Encrypt( String Key );
     boolean Decrypt( String Key );
}
```

If a class is created, which specifies `implements Securable`, then that class must provide the `Encrypt` and `Decrypt` functions to fulfill the requirements of the Securable interface.

Packages

A package is a group of classes, and is used to organize your source code. The keyword `package` at the start of a .java file declares the package name for the classes within the file. Multiple .java files may declare themselves a part of the same package.

Package names are usually implemented in dotted notation, and simulate a hierarchical structure. Packages starting with "java." are a code part of the Java environment (javax. is an exception, for the Swing components). Package names are also used to enable the use of two classes with the same name, as long as their package names differ.

By convention, companies creating their own packages usually use their internet domain names in reverse order, along with a description of the package itself. For example, `com.microsoft.sql` would be the package created by www.microsoft.com for their SQL JDBC driver. `Org.openroad.security` might be the package the www.openroad.org created for its security classes.

If you do not specify a package name in your .java file, then your classes are considered a part of the default package and have no package name. This is a very poor practice for anything but small test programs and classes. For example:

```
package org.openroad.security;

public class Crypt {
      boolean setKey( String Key ) {…};
      String getKey(){ … };
}
```

Using the `import` keyword, you are specifying which classes or packages you want to be able to refer to be their simple names. For example, without an import statement, the class above would be called `org.openroad.security.Crypt`. But, by including "import org.openroad.security.Crypt" in the program, the name would simply be `Crypt`. You can also use wildcards when declaring an import statement, to simply access to all classes at a specific level in the package, such as `import org.openroad.security.*;` to import all the openroad security classes.

In order for predefined classes to be used from their packages, you must also set up your CLASSPATH environment variable correctly. The CLASSPATH environment variable defines where the java compiler and the JRE are to look for user packages. The CLASSPATH value contains a list of directory names and/or jar file names.

In order to use the above class properly as a reusable class, you should do the following:

- Create the class and specify the proper package name.
- Compile the .java file, and create a .class file.

- Copy the .class file to a folder structure that mimics the package name. For example:

```
C:\MyJavaClasses\org\opernroad\security
```

- Set the CLASSPATH environment variable to point to the folder containing the root of the folder structure. Also include the "." Folder. For example:

```
SET CLASSPATH=C:\MyJavaClasses;
```

- Write a new program in a separate folder where the Crypt files do not exist. The code should look similar to the following:

```
import org.openroad.security.*;
public class MyApp {
public static void main( String[] args )
        {
                Crypt cr = new Crypt();
...
}
```

- The new application should compile and run cleanly, even though Crypt.class is not in the current folder.

NOTE: *If you alter the CLASSPATH variable, you should be sure to include the "." path (current directory) in its definition. Otherwise, classes in the current directory will not be identified by the JRE tools.*

Classes in C++

Creating a class in C++ is similar to creating a structure. Class objects have members just like a structure, but instead of just data, they also have code or functions as members. The basic template is this:

```
class ClassName
{
public:
        ClassName();        // Constructor
        ~ClassName();       //Destructor
private:
protected:
};
```

The `class` keyword begins the definition.

The `ClassName` becomes the name for the class, and is used later to create instances of it.

The `public` keyword defines a section where the members are visible or accessible to other objects or functions.

The `private` keyword defines a section where the members are invisible or nonaccessible to other objects or functions. This is the default if no access type is specified. This feature helps C++ implement data abstraction.

The `protected` keyword defines a section where the members are like `private`, except that they will be visible to other classes derived from this class.

Constructor and Destructor

Inside the `public` section just shown, the functions `ClassName` and `~ClassName` are defined (like in a prototype). These are the constructor and destructor for this class. The constructor is called whenever an instance of a class is created, and the destructor is called when the instance is destroyed.

NOTE: *The constructor and destructor are functions with the same name as the class, and have no return type. The destructor name is preceded with the tilde (~), and never accepts an argument. The constructor may be overloaded. Constructors and destructors are not required, but are most commonly implemented.*

Member Functions

In order to write any member function's body, it is usually done outside the definition (the only difference between regular functions and members is the presence of `ClassName::` as part of the name) in the following format:

```
ClassName::MemberFunction()
{
}
```

When a member function definition inside the class definition is followed by the `const` keyword, it means that the function will not change any of the (nonstatic) data members of that object. For instance:

```
class MDate {
public:
      bool IsValid() const;
private:
      int M, D, Y;
};
```

In the previous example, the `IsValid` member function of the MDate class has a `const` following its name and parameter list. This means that the code inside this function will not change any of the nonstatic data members, such as M, D, and Y.

Inline Functions

Inline functions can be created within the class definition, without the `inline` keyword. The format requires the function's body to follow the member definition:

```
class Example
{
public:
        Example();  // Constructor
        ~Example ();        // Destructor
        int IsExampleEmpty( void ) { return( IsEmpty ); };
    // Automatic
inline function
    private:
        int IsEmpty;
    };
```

Unions, Structs, and Classes

The similarities between unions, structures, and classes in C++ goes a little further then might be expected. In C++, unions and classes may also include the `protected`, `private`, and `public`, as well as constructors, destructors, and other member functions. In fact, the struct is converted into a class by the C++ compiler. The only difference between these types is that union and struct members are `public` by default, where in a class the default is `private`.

Objects and Functions, Copy Constructors

Objects can be passed as regular variables (or references or pointers) to functions, but some care must taken be taken. When an object is passed as a parameter, an exact copy of the object is made without invoking the object's constructor. On the other hand, the object's destructor is called for that copy when it is no longer needed.

Some objects (especially ones where memory is allocated) will not work properly under these conditions.

In order to eliminate this problem, a class must implement a *copy constructor*, a special constructor that takes as an argument a const reference to that same type. For example:

```
class Mobject
{
public:
     MObject();  // Regular constructor
     Mobject( const Mobject &Original );// Note Original is not a required
     name.
}
```

The copy constructor (instead of the default constructor) is called when an object is passed to a function, for autoinitialization, or when an object is returned from a function. It is not called during a normal assignment (you may write an overloaded operator to handle this). For example:

```
Foo( SomeObject );   // Copy constructor called to make a
     copy of SomeObject
MObject A = B;       // Copy ctor called for auto-initialization
     B is an
MObject  )
A = B;          // Copy constructor is NOT called.
```

Enums Inside Classes

You can place an enum definition within a class, and have the enum values follow the standard class access rules of private, public, and protected. Once defined, you access the enum as any other member, but for `public` members outside the class you must use the `scope resolution` operator:

```
#include <iostream>
class MDate
{
public:
     enum Day { Sun, Mon, Tue, Wed, Thu, Fri, Sat };
     MDate() { M=0; D=0; Y=0; WeekDay=Sun; };          //
Use 'Sun' constant value
     Day GetWeekDay( void ) { return( WeekDay ); };  //
Use 'Day' data type
private:
Day WeekDay;            // Use of Day data type
     char M, Y, D;
};
```

```
void main( void )
{
      MDate Today;
      MDate::Day D;              // Note scope resolution operator
      D = Today.GetWeekDay();
      if( D == MDate::Sun ) // Note scope resolution operator
            cout << "All is well\n";
}
```

Static Members

Static data members are members that exist only once, no matter how many instances of a class are created. These static members can be viewed almost like a global variable, except that they are accessed within an object. Remember that all objects (of the same or derived class) will share the same static member. You must declare the actual static variable outside the class definition—and inside. For example:

```
#include <iostream>

enum Modes { off, on };

void TurnStreetLights( int Mode )
{
      cout << "Traffic lights turned " << (Mode ? "on":"off")
   << endl;
}

class Cars
{
public:
      Cars() {
            if( CarsOnRoad == 0 )
                  TurnStreetLights( on );
            CarsOnRoad++; };
      ~Cars() {
            if( --CarsOnRoad == 0 )
                  TurnStreetLights( off );
            };
private:
      static int CarsOnRoad;  // This defines CarsOnRoads as static
};

int Cars::CarsOnRoad;        // Note 2nd declaration,
this is the actual variable
```

```
void main( void )
{
      Cars Me;
}
```

Functions within classes may also be static, in which case they can only access other static functions or static data members.

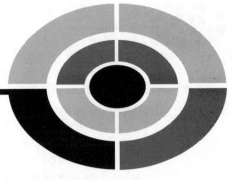

Class Definitions in C#

A C# class is defined in the following format:

```
[attributes] [modifiers] class identifier [:base-list] { class-body }[;]
```

where *attributes* may be one of the following:

- **public**   The class is available to all other pieces of code.
- **Internal**   The class is available only to other pieces of code in the same assembly.

NOTE: *Protected and* Private *are not permissible at the class definition level, except for nested classes.*

Modifiers may be

- **abstract**   The class is an abstract class, and can only be used as a base class for new classes.
- **sealed**   The class is a sealed class, and cannot be used as the base class of a new class.

The new keyword is not permissible at the class definition level, but is used to make members of a base class invisible to a derived class (new appears in the derived class).

The base-list is a list of base classes. Unlike C++ where a derived class defines the accessibility of its base class, the base class defines accessibility. For example, if a base class declared itself as internal, then a derived class would inherit the base classes members as internal.

A class can contain declarations of the following member types: constructors, destructors, constants, fields, methods, properties, indexers, and operators. Fields are common data members.

Properties are methods that define accessor functions for some value or property of the class. There is no property keyword; instead the declaration of the property appears in formatting the code:

```
public class Picture
{
        private int m_RotateAngle;
        public int RotateAngle
        {
            get{ return( m_RotateAngle ); }
            set{ if( value>=0 && value<=359) m_RotateAngle = value; }
        }
...
```

Indexers are methods that provide an index operator on the class. The special format of declaration is similar to a property, only it uses the this keyword in the declaration as the property name. For example:

```
public class Picture
{
    private int[] m_TagID;
    public int this[int Index] // Index can be of any data type.
    {
        set { if( Index >=0 && Index <= m_TagID.Length )
m_TagID[Index]=value; }
        get { if( Index >=0 && Index <= m_TagID.Length )
                    return(m_TagID[Index]); else return(-1);
        }
    }
...
```

Operator methods are operator overloads similar to those in C++. The main difference is that the methods must be declared *public static*, and all parameters are passed to them (unlike the implicit left-hand operator this in C++). An example of an operator would be the following:

```
Class Date {
     public static int operator+( Date D, int Days ) {...};
```

Destructors and Garbage Collection

Like Java, C# implements automatic garbage collection. Though a destructor can be
declared in C#, it is important to note that they are called when the Garbage Collector determines the object is no longer reachable by code, and when memory space is
needed.

A destructor has the same format in C# as in C++: ~ClassName();. The garbage collector will invoke this method automatically, when it sees fit.

In the event you are handling nonmanaged (non-CLR) resources, you may want to
force the garbage collection for the object. In order to do this, you must declare your
class to implement the IDispose interface, and also provide a Dispose method. A typical example is

```csharp
using System;
class Testing : IDisposable
{
  bool is_disposed = false;
  protected virtual void Dispose(bool disposing)
  {
    if (!is_disposed) // only dispose once!
    {
      if (disposing)
      {
            // Not in destructor, OK to reference other objects
      }
      // perform cleanup for this object
    }
    this.is_disposed = true;
  }
  public void Dispose()
  {
    Dispose(true);
    // tell the GC not to finalize
    GC.SuppressFinalize(this);
  }
  ~Testing()
  {
    Dispose(false);
  }
}
```

Assemblies

An assembly implements the following set of information for one or more code files:

- **Versioning**   Group modules that should have the same version information.
- **Deployment**   Group code modules and resources that support your model of deployment.
- **Reuse**   Group modules if they can be used together logically for some purpose. For example, an assembly consisting of types and classes used infrequently for program maintenance can be put in the same assembly. In addition, types that you intend to share with multiple applications should be grouped into an assembly and the assembly should be signed with a strong name.
- **Security**   Group modules containing types that require the same security permissions.
- **Scoping**   Group modules containing types whose visibility should be restricted to the same assembly.

Assemblies are nothing more than text files similar to source code. They can be embedded within a CLR-executable program, or defined outside the CLR for multiple files. Many programs can include an assembly in the single executable files. The following is a brief example of an Assembly for a C# project:

```
using System.Reflection;
using System.Runtime.CompilerServices;

[assembly: AssemblyTitle("")]
[assembly: AssemblyDescription("")]
[assembly: AssemblyConfiguration("")]
[assembly: AssemblyCompany("")]
[assembly: AssemblyProduct("")]
[assembly: AssemblyCopyright("")]
[assembly: AssemblyTrademark("")]
[assembly: AssemblyCulture("")]
[assembly: AssemblyVersion("1.0.*")]
[assembly: AssemblyDelaySign(false)]
[assembly: AssemblyKeyFile("")]
[assembly: AssemblyKeyName("")]
```

INDEX

INTERNATIONAL CONTACT INFORMATION

AUSTRALIA
McGraw-Hill Book Company
Australia Pty. Ltd.
TEL +61-2-9900-1800
FAX +61-2-9878-8881
http://www.mcgraw-hill.com.au
books-it_sydney@mcgraw-hill.com

CANADA
McGraw-Hill Ryerson Ltd.
TEL +905-430-5000
FAX +905-430-5020
http://www.mcgraw-hill.ca

**GREECE, MIDDLE EAST, & AFRICA
(Excluding South Africa)**
McGraw-Hill Hellas
TEL +30-210-6560-990
TEL +30-210-6560-993
TEL +30-210-6560-994
FAX +30-210-6545-525

MEXICO (Also serving Latin America)
McGraw-Hill Interamericana Editores
S.A. de C.V.
TEL +525-1500-5108
FAX +525-117-1589
http://www.mcgraw-hill.com.mx
carlos_ruiz@mcgraw-hill.com

SINGAPORE (Serving Asia)
McGraw-Hill Book Company
TEL +65-6863-1580
FAX +65-6862-3354
http://www.mcgraw-hill.com.sg
mghasia@mcgraw-hill.com

SOUTH AFRICA
McGraw-Hill South Africa
TEL +27-11-622-7512
FAX +27-11-622-9045
robyn_swanepoel@mcgraw-hill.com

SPAIN
McGraw-Hill/
Interamericana de España, S.A.U.
TEL +34-91-180-3000
FAX +34-91-372-8513
http://www.mcgraw-hill.es
professional@mcgraw-hill.es

**UNITED KINGDOM, NORTHERN,
EASTERN, & CENTRAL EUROPE**
McGraw-Hill Education Europe
TEL +44-1-628-502500
FAX +44-1-628-770224
http://www.mcgraw-hill.co.uk
emea_queries@mcgraw-hill.com

ALL OTHER INQUIRIES Contact:
McGraw-Hill/Osborne
TEL +1-510-420-7700
FAX +1-510-420-7703
http://www.osborne.com
omg_international@mcgraw-hill.com

The fast and easy way to understanding computing fundamentals

- *No formal training needed*
- *Self-paced, easy-to-follow, and user-friendly*
- *Amazing low price*

0-07-225454-8
Available May 2004

0-07-225363-0
Available April 2004

0-07-225514-5
Available July 2004

0-07-225359-2
Available March 2004

0-07-225370-3
Available May 2004

0-07-225364-9
Available March 2004

For more information on these and other McGraw-Hill/Osborne titles, visit www.osborne.com.

Complete
Your Shelf

Expert authors, comprehensive coverage, timely topics...Complete References

C#:
The Complete Reference
Herbert Schildt
0-07-213485-2

J2EE™:
The Complete Reference
Jim Keogh
0-07-222472-X

Business Objects:
The Complete Reference
Cindi Howson
0-07-222681-1

Java™ 2:
The Complete Reference,
Fifth Edition
Herbert Schildt
0-07-222420-7

Crystal Reports® 9:
The Complete Reference
George Peck
0-07-222519-X

SQL:
The Complete Reference,
Second Edition
James Groff & Paul Weinberg
0-07-222559-4

Know How

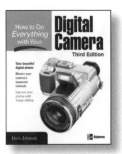

How to Do Everything with Your Digital Camera
Third Edition
ISBN: 0-07-223081-9

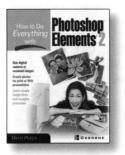

How to Do Everything with Photoshop Elements 2
ISBN: 0-07-222638-2

How to Do Everything with Photoshop CS
ISBN: 0-07-223143-2
4-color

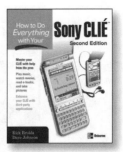

How to Do Everything with Your Sony CLIÉ
Second Edition
ISBN: 0-07-223074-6

How to Do Everything with Macromedia Contribute
0-07-222892-X

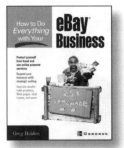

How to Do Everything with Your eBay Business
0-07-222948-9

How to Do Everything with Illustrator CS
ISBN: 0-07-223092-4
4-color

How to Do Everything with Your iPod
ISBN: 0-07-222700-1

How to Do Everything with Your iMac,
Third Edition
ISBN: 0-07-213172-1

How to Do Everything with Your iPAQ Pocket
Second Edition
ISBN: 0-07-222950-0

Sound Off!

Visit us at **www.osborne.com/bookregistration** and let us know what you thought of this book. While you're online you'll have the opportunity to register for newsletters and special offers from McGraw-Hill/Osborne.

We want to hear from you!

Sneak Peek

Visit us today at **www.betabooks.com** and see what's coming from McGraw-Hill/Osborne tomorrow!

Based on the successful software paradigm, Bet@Books™ allows computing professionals to view partial and sometimes complete text versions of selected titles online. Bet@Books™ viewing is free, invites comments and feedback, and allows you to "test drive" books in progress on the subjects that interest you the most.